BEHIND THE COMIC MASK

Behind the comic mask is truth

BEHIND THE COMIC MASK

Sam Kershen

The Book Guild Ltd
Sussex, England

To Marty

This book is sold subject to the condition that it shall not, by way of trade or otherwise, be lent, re-sold, hired out, photocopied or held in any retrieval system or otherwise circulated without the publisher's prior consent in any form of binding or cover other than that in which this is published and without a similar condition including this condition being imposed on the subsequent purchaser.

The Book Guild Ltd
25 High Street,
Lewes, Sussex

First published 1996
© Sam Kershen, 1996

Set in Palatino
Typesetting by Acorn Bookwork, Salisbury

Printed in Great Britain by
Antony Rowe Ltd, Chippenham, Wiltshire.

A catalogue record for this book is available from the British Library

ISBN 1 85776 069 7

CONTENTS

1	A Mixed Bunch, Pot or no Pot	7
2	Making an Old Man Happy	17
3	'It's Not Cricket'	19
4	Cricket Boots and Teenage Dreams	23
5	'If You Don't Come Home on Saturday, Don't Come Home on Sunday'	27
6	Mens Sana in Corpore Sano and all That Codswallop	32
7	Aspects of the Way We Were	46
8	Mayonnaise is in the Eye of the Beholder	54
9	Our Part in the History of the World	61
10	What The Paper Says	72
11	The Birds are Singing and I Hear Gypsy Violins When You Smile at Me	78
12	The Truth About Professor Einstein and his Mates	88
13	A Kick in the Vanities	94
14	La Plume de ma Tante	102
15	What's in a Name – And Who Cares?	111
16	Poverty is no Crime, But it's Better to be Rich Than Poor	119
17	The Shocking Case of the Korean Swordfish	124

18	A Nose by any Other Name	129
19	Pauncefoot's Last Stand	136
20	Do Pubs Sell Wallpaper?	144
21	Retired, Deeply Hurt	153
22	A Pride of Trenchermen	164
23	Sex and Sleaze	173

1

A MIXED BUNCH, POT OR NO POT

I have discovered the satisfaction and the feeling of being at one with the rest of society, that flow from being a part of a group of people, one of a team, who share their interests and have themselves something to contribute to the intercourse essential for the promotion of speech and thought. Thus it is that I have had the good fortune of becoming a member of a few clubs or societies that have rewarded me with a special kind of camaraderie. Foremost has been the company of my fellow alumni of Owen's School from which I have derived some of the happiest times of my life, wherein all kinds of persons of all degrees of society become part of such a team and rub shoulders together.

Another is the Agora Society where extremes meet, peers and paupers, the wealthy and the indigent, sophisticates on the one hand and vulgarians on the other, all with their own peculiar qualities and each a story unto himself.

When, on the occasion of the 150th anniversary of the foundation of the Agora Society this week, an ancient and honourable society, I sat back and took stock. I was full of wonderment at the remarkable collection of my confrères. The society was founded in 1845 by a 'group of gentlemen from the City of London', limited to a maximum of 60 members all of whom must be resident or engaged in the earning of their living in the City. Nominees must be 'clubbable' and prepared to meet four times in the year to dine privately, to hear guest speakers and 'to engage restfully and confidentially in intercourse on the topics of the time'. An anachronism perhaps, but for some, bachelors, widowers or abandoned spouses, an oasis in an otherwise lonely existence, and an opportunity for social and political ideas, anecdotes and unmalicious chaff, with cronies we would never meet in the ordinary course.

The dinners are held in a private room at the Imperial Hotel and I have had the opportunity and the time to grow to know my fellow travellers quite intimately. How disparate and unusual a bunch they are, deserving of recording for posterity. As was said by a well-known member of another club, 'no one gives a bugger if you haven't a pot to pee in'. Need I say, the chap who said this had the biggest pot in the land and was reputedly the most seriously rich member of the House of Lords. We have here a collection of men from different backgrounds, fastidiously correct yet each in his own way worthy of close study. Correct, because they are quintessentially and archetypically British. As Lenin is reported to have said pertinently, 'if they [the English] planned to storm a railway station they would all buy platform tickets first.' He might well have had the Agora lot in mind. Some might justifiably characterize them as a self-satisfied clique of die-hard Brits. There is no record that a member has ever been expelled; on the rare occasion that one has 'overstepped the mark', some undefined wondrous process seems to move into action and it is not long before he offers his resignation, usually quoting a specious personal pretext.

Raymond, the secretary this past 20 years, rules with a rod of iron, a porcine fellow, bucolic in appearance with a hairstyle, mutton-chop whiskers and general facial fungus that looks as if someone had stabbed a sofa; with the best will in the world he could only merit the description volunteered by one of the younger and less reverent members, namely as looking like a Maltese ponce. With snout thrust forward, I am reminded of the tale told of him, on the basis of the old music hall sally, of when he recently entered the room with a dog under his arm. Another member is said to have asked, 'Who's the pig you're with?' and Raymond said, 'That's not a pig, that's a dog,' to which the other retorted, 'I was talking to the dog.'

Most of the members are of pensionable age and some have to rely on sticks for locomotion. The oldest inhabitant and elder statesman is Bagshaw. We don't know how old he is but I'm sure that if he were a horse he'd have to be shot. He is a bore of the first order, ex-county cricketer and a prominent racehorse owner; he still relies on a shooting stick on which he perches while banging on to the rest of us with his lengthy lectures of the 'Disgusted of Tunbridge Wells' variety. He does not suffer fools or for that matter anyone else gladly. It seems curious but it was many years ago that I suggested irritably to him a course to take with the handle of his bat and only now, 20 years later, is the old buffer taking my advice with his stick, not his bat. The stick tends to slip on the polished floor; how ironic it would be if, like Edward II of England, he met his end (so to say) in a peculiarly appropriate manner.

Bagshaw's interest is now exclusively focused on the horse-racing scene and it is reported that he recently walked out of church angrily because the parson prayed for fine weather when Bagshaw's colt needed the mud. He has a fund of stories including the one of his trainer who furiously demanded of his jockey, 'I thought I told you to stay in touch till the straight, then quicken and go to the front.' 'I would have,' came the reply, 'but I had to stay with the horse.'

Then, at the other end of the scale, there is our treasurer, Walter. Walter is a sidesman and as righteous, abstemious and dull a citizen as you could possibly fear to meet. He advocates penal measures to mulct the 'profiteer' with changes in the VAT laws. He advocates a tax on everything, potato crisps, thimbles, paper hankies and budgies' food and is presently agitating for large fines on Sunday traders and immediate arrest without trial for non-payment. He's the kind of chap who would empower the police to break into your home to see if you've used a garden hose and would enthusiastically sponsor a bill for automatic explosion of a device attached to your thigh if you've drunk more than two pints.

I find it hard to believe Raymond's story that he saw the holier-than-thou Walter coming out of the Girlie Strip Club in Old Compton Street last week, looking very shaky and worse for wear after the adult entertainment offered him. It matches the case of the man who was reported to have absconded from his old people's home to celebrate his 100th birthday with a trip to London one afternoon. 'I went to the pictures and saw a French film,' he explained, 'but it was full of nudes and after three hours I walked out.' But you never know. And although I do not wish to seem unduly suspicious, what was Raymond himself doing in Old Compton Street anyway – social work?

Another outstanding character is Hugh, a circuit judge and a former Oxford cricket blue. Hugh is a jovial swashbuckling type with panache, likeable but indigent. He is an authority on the sporting scene and is currently seething on the quality of the umpiring with which our touring side has had to contend in Australia; his expressed opinion is that most of the umpires must have been kinsmen of the Spanish royal family – they are terrible bleeders, he says. He has little empathy with most of our colleagues for their sporting allegiance is blindly and overwhelmingly to golf and they are about as interested and knowledgable in cricket as Yoko Ono – and that's not saying much. He is a bachelor but with a keen eye for a complaisant woman and it is thought that some of the most beautiful ladies of London society have shared his bed. He says he recently received a letter from a gentleman who accused him of an affair with his wife. He says he wrote in reply, 'Thank you for your circular letter.'

Guy is a retired scientist, meticulously but insufferably precise, with only one eye and as deaf as a post. Perhaps understandably he is a little eccentric. On hearing that Hugh still turns out for the village cricket club, he's been trying for some time to warn him of the truth of the theory propounded in a Swedish scientific journal that the unnatural heat caused by the wearing of white trousers has a cumulatively serious effect on the male organ. It is believed that he is such a perfectionist that he has a spare bloodshot glass eye to wear if he has a cold. He is stubborn and a know-all; among other things, he claims to have seen evidence that the landing on the moon was faked and is an active member of the Flat Earth Society.

Cyril, a mild unworldly chap who looks like the elder Steptoe, is an accomplished church organist and lives and breathes music. Hugh says of him that he even blows his nose in the key of G. He cuts a rather forlorn figure and always looks as if he's just emerged from a hard night in a cave. In the sartorial area we think he must be dressed by Patrick Moore's tailor.

Trevor was a rubber planter in Malaysia until he joined up in World War II. After distinguished and heroic service he was awarded the Military Cross but was taken prisoner and suffered badly in a Japanese POW camp, losing a leg. He is bitter about the brutal treatment he barely survived. He is a large fellow but now in poor health. He claims that this is due to a post-malarial syndrome but we think it is down to a drink problem – he can't get enough; a case of a chronic disorder known as a permanent insufficiency of alcohol in the blood. He is agreeable to everyone except when he's in drink, which is nearly all the time, and was heard to observe thickly, after the last dinner in which he copiously put away a punishing quantity, that all he wants out of life is a round of squash and a glass of billiards.

An itinerant second-line actor is the diminutive and charming Cliff. He has known better days and sadly, is not destined to achieve fame on the boards. He is a very superstitious fellow and when he boasts of his past successes, as he often does, he tells that he was once offered the star role in the musical of 'Abraham Lincoln' but refused because he was scared he'd be assassinated on the way to the theatre. He swears that when he was playing the Prince in *Hamlet* many years ago he had many complimentary notices including one from an American who wrote to say that he was bringing his wife and could Cliff work into his lines 'Happy Birthday Florence.' Now, he is confined to 'bit' engagements (if that is an apt description of the rear end of a horse which he played in his last job in the Smethwick panto production at Christmas). His payments of subscriptions and dining fees suffer from an inbuilt inconsistency but he is popular and an entertaining companion and calls everyone 'Luvvie'. His language and the brand of his scatological stories would be the envy of a Billingsgate porter and get him two years without the option if uttered publicly. While the rest of us chortle if Walter is within earshot, his face takes on a deep crimson hue that makes me fear an incipient brain haemorrhage. I think it was in deference to Walter's sensibilities that the committee turned down Cliff's suggestion for introducing topless waitresses into the dinners. One of his tales is of the stripper who collapsed on the stage halfway through her act; an ambulance was called and she was taken to hospital. The doctors there examined her and found that her G-string was too tight. His punch-line is that they sent for a piano tuner. When he first told this one, Walter exited with a very bad coughing fit.

The bald-headed Rupert is also full of interesting stories. He has a fund of reminiscences including the story of the BBC programme some years ago in which Malcolm Muggeridge interviewed Brendan Behan and throughout which Behan called him Buggeridge. Sixteen listeners telephoned to offer sinus remedies for Behan.

Rupert was originally a BBC producer but is now a drama critic, probably the most powerful in the land. It is said that a bad notice from him can close a play after one night. Cliff has the story of a prominent theatrical producer who saw Rupert in his seat at a recent opening and gave him a kiss on his bald head. Another man in the stalls shouted out, 'Wrong end'.

He was once the target for an attempt on his life by a playwright whose *oeuvre* he had given a savage slating, when the aggrieved writer had used his car to pin Rupert against the railings in Regents Park; only a low kerb prevented serious injury. Rupert's autocracy does not extend to his home where he has a tempestuous domestic existence; his fourth marriage is with a woman half his age, an actress well known as a volatile Mexican spitfire. He invariably sports scratches and bruises when he appears and one evening last winter he arrived bent almost double just as if he'd been kicked in the wotsits. He explained that he'd collided with a door. With his genitals?

With such a high incidence of members of mature years, it is useful to have a doctor in our midst and in fact we have two. One is Lionel, with a Harley Street address, a small dapper man who always wears a spotted bow tie. He is well known to have a busy slimming practice, especially with ladies in the theatrical field. An unplanned appearance before the General Medical Council a few years back called a temporary halt in his activity while suspended for 12 months after charges of professional misconduct. Allegations of drug addiction were made by a number of his patients who had been supplied with generous quantities of amphetamine tablets for weight reduction, without prior examination. Indeed, they testified that they had been supplied in many cases solely in response to an advertisement inviting postal applications. The tabloid press had a field-day, of course, and Lionel was considered lucky to have been penalized with a mere suspension.

Lionel is particularly thick with another of our number who has had a brush with the authorities, Kevin. Kevin is as slippery as a sliced mango and used to boast of his important work as a leading British film producer but a prosecution for supply of obscene material, namely pornographic videos, hit the tabloid press a few years ago and blew the gaff. He was reported to have supplied the offending material by mail order and a delicatessen keeper in Wigan who was dissatisfied with his order complained to the police. The court was asked to say that the videos, which among other unusual features depicted scenes of a housewife performing unnameable acts with a Hoover and a hard-boiled egg, were calculated to deprave or corrupt those likely to see them. In the event, the jury, perhaps slightly fuddled after viewing a large number of spectacular exhibits, refused to find for the prosecution and Kevin was acquitted, but not before he'd lost some of his bounce. He now follows a more exalted vocation of selling property time-shares.

There are many others who merit a mention. The second medical man is Stefan, a gynaecologist originally from Vienna and a concentration camp survivor. We always know if he's been operating when he arrives at dinner, because his thick-lensed glasses are invariably spattered with blood. His reputation is slightly tarnished through an unfortunate habit of leaving swabs in his patients' insides. His last lapse of memory cost him a mere £25,000 in damages; in America, the damages awarded would have been at least $10 million. That he suffers seriously with halitosis is only too evident when he is in conversation in close proximity. Worse, it's no use crinkling your nose and turning your head away to escape his breath because he will follow it around so that the full blast is always trained on your face.

Benno, Swiss, is a philanthropist, who quietly but generously funds many worthy artistic and charitable projects from what is reputed to be an immense fortune. He is ailing, having survived three heart by-pass operations. He has been advised that he is unable to support a fourth and his arterial condition is such that his doctor's prognosis is bleak. A messy and fiercely contested divorce is not helping.

'Kipper', an actuary, is so called because of his propensity to doze off in the midst of the proceedings; he disgraced himself by falling asleep during a very interesting talk by the guest speaker of the evening, Sir Huw Wheldon. His stentorian snoring was halted in short order when Bagshaw gave him a vicious prod in the ribs with his stick. He distinguished himself by disappearing altogether another evening and it was only when the alarm was raised by his wife that he was found asleep, strange to relate, in the ladies' loo some hours after we'd all gone home.

George is a distinguished stock market analyst, who can't quite explain the arcane dividing line between on the one hand, his plumbing for profit and dividend information from public company directors to pass on to his clients, and, on the other, information illegally gained and used for 'insider trading'. I do not wish to be uncharitable but I can't help saying that rather than rely on George's expertise I would sooner put my savings in the old brown teapot.

Then there is Sebastian, heavily bearded and silent and sullenly inscrutable, behind dark glasses, purporting to be a security officer. Could he be Lord Lucan, we wonder? We'll never know because he recently resigned quite suddenly. He didn't say if he wanted to spend more time with his family, and departed unmourned.

Among the ruck there are a peer of the realm, a brace of minor politicians, an honest accountant, a sprinkling of solicitors and a token alcoholic newspaperman, each one with his own peculiar story of his inside life. Of strange happenings like the curious case of the cloakroom thefts when Peter's spare set of false teeth went missing, of the brawl involving a near strangling attack between the extreme right wing Palmerston-minded Trevor and the liberal-minded Rudy, and of the embarrassing blackballing of an Indian textile magnate that split the membership of the Society and threatened a break-up, there must be another chronicle and a further study awaits. But the sanctity of our well-loved institution must not be compromised; we must be constantly on our guard for the desideratum that it withstands the pressures for, if not, as someone said, like going bald or being cuckolded, it will be too late to do anything about it.

By the way, the names have been changed. In case you think you recognize any of the individuals portrayed in this essay, I would like to take the precaution of claiming that, you may believe it or not, all characters are fictitious and any resemblance to persons, living or dead, is purely coincidental. I can do without any writs for libel, thank you.

2

MAKING AN OLD MAN HAPPY

I am just returned from California where I have to report that one does not find too many Old Owenians in really powerful back-stabbing positions in the entertainment world. In fact, I found things in Hollywood getting so rough that the boys are stabbing each other in the front these days. Keeping up appearances there is expensive – it costs $50 a day to rent a bowler hat. And American TV is so bad that it is reported that husbands are beginning to talk to wives.

It was, therefore, pleasing indeed to find Old Owenian Jessica Tandy, receiving a Motion Picture Academy Golden Award, with her husband Hume Cronyn, for distinction in the acting profession over the past 50 years. The presentation was one of the most popular ever.

But back in this old country, I was recently myself on the receiving end of an accolade that I rank among the most pleasurable ever accorded me. (True, this is not an area where there are many contenders). The other day, at one of the so agreeable pre-Christmas lunches masterminded at its academic Wandsworth venue by that genial keeper of Owenian history and the guardian of its alumni consciousness, Harold Moore, I met Frank Mussett, a distinguished Old Owenian. At the luncheon, I passed among such disparate characters as Doug Young, John Turner, Ken Attrill and many other notorious citizens.

Frank and I had never met before but it was not long before I perceived in him the good taste and percipience that characterize Old Owenians, wherever they are to be found. This was demonstrated when he told me that he had been away in Singapore for, I think, some 25 years and that he had always looked forward to receiving the *Old Owenian* or the *Mark* out there to derive entertainment and nostalgic pleasure from reading the pieces I had myself written over a period of years. Clearly, I was right; here was a man of considerable judgement.

Now, I do not know whether to attribute to Frank a remarkable quality of literary discernment or, as Jim Everton will hazard, some sign of mental deterioration but I must admit to a warm sense of pride which diffused my normal humility, to think that my modest (I know, modesty is the fig-leaf of mediocrity, Harold) writings had been awaited and read as if they were worthy of the trouble by an Old Owenian on important duties 15,000 miles away (or is it 10,000? I think I hear Jesse Smith stirring in his grave) let alone by my contemporary middle-aged citizens in North London who, if truth is told, still confine their reading to the centrefolds of certain colourful publications.

So, thank you, Frank Mussett, for making an Old Owenian happy. May you and I derive pleasurable intercourse (social), pace Harold Moore, at Wandsworth for many years yet.

3

'IT'S NOT CRICKET'

In the course of 13 completed innings this year, I have amassed a grand total of 17 runs, a batting average of 1.3 and the time has come for action. I've been on the receiving end of his machiavellian tricks for too long and enough is enough.

I don't know what the man I am seeking looks like. What I do know is that he is devilishly cunning, resourceful and he's dedicated himself to the destruction of my career on the cricket field. In the months since last May, he has popped up all over the place, never failing to go into action whenever and wherever the matches take place. A last-minute change of venue never foxes him.

Versatile to a fault, he's never at a loss for a means of achieving his purpose. Last weekend, for instance, returned fit from a holiday in the sun, full of confidence and seeing the ball as big as a house, as they say, I went to the wicket with eight of my side's wickets down and needing only four runs to win the game. With two elderly, slowish bowlers to face I was serenely confident, but as I took guard and looked down the pitch I saw that he'd struck again. He'd got the captain of the opposing side to bring back the opening fast bowler again, a mountain of a man, a vicious barbarian with a matted beard and barrel chest and a speed of body-line delivery for which he should have faced a charge of aggravated assault; certainly the MCC should have declared his conduct against public policy. I fidgeted and resurveyed the disposition of the field with deliberate exhaustiveness as long as I thought possible without provoking an appeal for dismissal on the grounds of time-wasting, and then settled to receive the bowling. A cold fearful hand clutched at my stomach as he thundered up to the crease. I thought he actually screamed like a Bulgarian shot-putter as his arm came over to deliver the ball but they told me afterwards that the sound came from me. In any case, as I knew it would be, his arm extended skyward well above the sight-screen which was designed to provide a contrasting background and I saw nothing whatever of the ball. A second or so later there was the clatter of falling wood and I made my way back to the pavilion. The last man in, a callow lad, had been played for his bowling and had never before scored a single run, hit a four and won the game to come back to generous applause that should have been mine.

On the morning of the match Old Boys v the School, always reckoned to be good for an easy twenty runs or so against the immature and erratic bowling of the youngsters, the man somehow got into my house and took the protective cup out of my cricket bag and hid it. The theft only became apparent later when I was putting on my batting pads and it was too late to do anything about it. The very first ball I received from the cocky little swine at the top end, a fourteen-year-old who fancied himself as a budding Fred Trueman, struck me full pitch in the very abdominal area for which the protective gear had been invented and I was carried off to the pavilion, gasping for breath, humiliated and certain that permanent damage had been caused to my marital performance.

Sometimes, the fellow gets complete strangers to help him. One perfect balmy Saturday in July when I was feeling strong and resolute, determined to add to the already handsome total amassed by my colleagues against a demoralized opposition, he timed his intervention beautifully. As I strode athletically towards the wicket, immaculately clad and sure I had him this time, he gave the signal to a local market gardener to light a bonfire. The smoke billowed across the pitch, so thick and acrid that it was as much as I could do to find my way to the crease, let alone see the one straight ball delivered before it arrived safely amid my stumps.

My persecutor has excellent connections. Money seems to be no object. He frequently hires an aircraft from a local airfield to fly low over the cricket field with very ancient and noisy World War II planes as I take my stance. I know that he drives a fast car because on one brilliantly sunny day in June, he parked at the edge of the field directly opposite my end of the pitch so that the sun was reflected blindingly in his windscreen and I suffered a migraine with partial blindness for the rest of the afternoon. As I groped my way back to the pavilion without having troubled the scorer, I didn't wait to change and hurried off to the car park intent on a confrontation but the car was gone. I know he was back in the neighbourhood that evening though, because just as it came to my turn to buy a round of drinks, he sent in four of my old school contemporaries who said they were unexpectedly and coincidentally in the district. They all ordered double brandies.

Sometimes when it is my turn to bat he arranges that the ball is lost and gives the bowler a substitute ball that is out of shape so that it isn't where it should be when I play forward. As it pitches, it breaks sharply away from my bat.

He has a bizarre sense of fun. Once in May, he actually got my fellow batsman at the other end to strike the ball hard towards me, hit me brutally and agonizingly on the ankle and go on to break my wicket before I could hobble back to my crease.

Eager and fit early in the season, I always used to start with a good score or two but it was on a very cold day in May this year that he contrived to have me put out of action for an entire week after he'd had a ball deal me a savage blow on the kneecap. The impact was so powerful and the pain, even through the pad, so great that I was bereft of speech for the rest of the day and, even after the temporary obstruction by my knee, the ball sped to the boundary.

I think I know what the man's after. I suppose he is one of those nuts who feel that it is wrong, socially or morally, to continue playing cricket after you are sixty years old and decrepit. He's damned clever but even if I don't find him, I will beat him. Even if I have to change my name, join another club and bat left-handed. After all, it might be an improvement.

4

CRICKET BOOTS AND TEENAGE DREAMS

In the last year before I left school in the 1930s my cricket boots cost me 7s 6d. A pair, I mean. At the time I thought it a prudent lifetime investment but how wrong I was.

I shook the dust of Owen's School from my feet with heavy heart and a damn great lump in my throat. Contrary to rumours put about by the likes of Dallas Rose, I was not invited to leave. True, I think that Jimmy Cracknell viewed the prospect of my staying on in the sixth as about as attractive as a colonic irrigation. He had been heard to say, 'That lad should go far – the farther the better.' Another member of the staff, not Headmaster Harry Newbitt Asman, had been heard to suggest that I was incapable of organizing a knees-up in a brewery (at least I think that's what he said) and Ben Morgan questioned my ability to run a whelk stall on Christmas Eve.

So, armed extraordinarily with a number of 'O' Levels including distinctions in English, Maths and Mechanics (a shock result from which I think that Jock Rees never recovered and which later sent him into some sort of decline), I gave notice. I had nearly always been the smallest in class and so my particular friends had been Terry Steele, Percy Cook and Noel Brunner; I cultivated them because they were the only ones smaller than me. I liked Percy Cook most of all because he was very much smaller than me. I was also quite friendly with a French boy whose name was Marcel Guenin or Guerin but I cannot remember his exact name because we used to call him

'*Merde*'; every second word he uttered was *Merde*! He couldn't wrap his tongue round the word Kershen so he used to call me *Cochon*.

I had had two main interests. One was cricket. In this I was encouraged unusually by 'Flash Pete' Hardwick, a mentor to whom I owed a great deal and whose sardonic *sturm und drang* concealed a consummate teaching ability and a civilized sensitivity. My cricketing enthusiasm was also sparked by my devotion to the Middlesex side and in particular as a worshipper of Hendren, Hearne, Allen, Durston, Enthoven et al. Sadly, things have changed and my game has now been affected by what is known to me and other talented cricketers like myself in mid-life crisis as the Mole Syndrome. It involves a mole bush telegraph system organized so that as soon as the moles hear that Kershen is at the crease they send along the mob to set up a small hill on the wicket just about on a good length. The deflections tend to baffle my bat. The mole mafia also advertise that any spot just in front of where I'm fielding is safe for a bit of fun at my expense. I appreciate that moles don't get too much fun because the experts tell us that they mate only once every 17 years; just the same, I wish they'd find another fall guy.

But back to the central question of cricket boots and whether new boots would improve my game. According to the actuaries (you know, an actuary is a chap who found accountancy too exciting), when consulted in regard to whether or not I ought to buy a new pair of cricket boots, they opined that my life expectancy measured against the likely term of my cricketing future was an equation too fine for mortal computation. True, my present boots, circa 1958, are showing signs of wear. For one thing the buttons are loose (and I'm taking this up with the manufacturer). Buttonhooks are hard to find. So when after much agonizing I did decide to invest in a new pair of boots, I called at Lillywhite's the other day, prepared if necessary to spend up to £1.50 with inflation in mind. Thus it was that I learned what other Old Owenians may have discovered, namely that it is no longer possible to buy a pint of beer, a packet of fags and a bag of crisps and still have change out of a shilling. At any rate, the assistant at Lillywhite's mouthed some outrageous prices such as £25 and so on and when I begged him to spare me the jokes, silently rolled his eyes heavenward. Refusing to lose my composure, I drew myself up to my full height and stared him in the crotch. After all, £25, like a German joke, is no laughing matter. 'Thank you,' I said. 'I'll try Tesco's Home 'n Wear.' I turned on my heel and would have made a dignified exit had it not been that I tripped on a nearby pole that whipped back smartly and dealt me a savage blow on the left knee. Numb with pain as I limped out of the store, I asked myself if this was a signal from the Greatest Cricket Bootseller in the Sky, counselling me to stand fast with my 1958 boots. Perhaps a hint that new boots might turn out an unwise extravagance?

I have referred the dilemma to other members of the club but have received no useful advice. Ivan Waterman and Ken Rowswell both made absurd and objectionable, not to say impractical, suggestions as to what I might do with my old bat. Talk about flannelled fools and muddied oafs; they're both on permanent vacation from the neck up.

*

Oh, you'd like to know of my other main interest at school? Well, that was connected with the opposite sex – to be precise, women. To be even more precise, the girls of Owen's School, who were forever in my thoughts. I was a shy lad (I heard that guffaw, Gerry Jones) and my fantasies were centred on the girls to be seen exiting in the afternoons from the school on the other side of the playground. There was the small round figure of Becky Leffel (I had discovered her name from a lucky swine who lived near her and knew her well enough to speak to) who would emerge at about a quarter to four, clad in black gymslip, dark-eyed and, to me, unbelievably voluptuous. I'd have given a year's beer money if she'd even thrown me a glance. But she didn't and although I often hovered at the Angel tram stop, feigning not to look her way, I never even got to speak to her. And Eileen Large, who had a brother at Owen's, was another. A statuesque girl, fair with blue eyes and deep brown complexion, I fantasised that one day she would cross the playground, boldly walk up to me and ask if I would treat her to a beans-on-toast tea at the Lyons' Corner House at the Angel. And then, who knows what might follow? It never happened and I doubt if she even knew that I existed. She did once cross the playground and, as we passed in Owen Street, hope flickered for a brief instant as she looked my way. I remember that I was reduced to a quivering jelly and with heart pounding, a small choking sound came from my throat as I gave out what I wanted to be a friendly smile; in fact, I realize now that wild-eyed, with my teeth bared like fangs and facial muscles rigid with terror, I must have presented as a weird slavering idiot and given the poor girl a terrible fright, because she sped away in the direction of the Stoke Newington bus stop. For a whole week, I sweated with fear, waiting to be summoned to the Headmaster's study to answer a complaint which Eileen would surely make about being accosted by a small creature, half boy and half monster. I was ready to confess and plead insanity and I considered the alternative of suicide but no call came.

So, deeply scarred by non-experience with these two *femmes fatales*, I thought it over and decided that women weren't worth it and I must give them up. I did not succeed in this resolve but that is another story.

By the way, about the boots, I think I've got the answer. Is anyone interested in leasing me a pair on a weekly basis?

5

'IF YOU DON'T COME HOME ON SATURDAY, DON'T COME HOME ON SUNDAY'

More than two years have passed since the demise of our ground at Whetstone, for over 60 years, without eleemosynary aid, a sporting and cultural centre of blessed and loving memory. As I look back over a half century or more, I see gratefully that all life was there.

In the pavilion, there were men and women, mostly macho but with only an occasional few who wouldn't go anywhere without their blow-driers, congregating to form a complete cross-section of society that could be relied on to disseminate good conversation that was wide ranging and never dull, a decent level of intellectual stimulation and well-informed sporting analysis. All were backed by a well-stocked bar with fine ale. If the loutish sometimes appeared, they tended wonderfully either to mellow or in the alternative to disappear fairly smartly.

One recalls nostalgically so many memorable successes on and off the field, broken promises and failures, friendships, intrigues, life partnerships forged, marriages broken; there was comradeship and romance and occasionally pain or despair. A microcosm of Owenian lifestyles was woven there.

And who among us can forget the lazy afternoons lounging in deck-chairs on the green in front of the pavilion to the sound of willow on leather and the muted cries of appealing out in the middle, our vista framed by patches of trees in the soft distance.

For all of us who had the vast good fortune of having passed through the doors of Owen's School, whether brilliant or ne'er-do-well, talented or pathetic, we each had the chance of making good friends for life.

Back in the dressing-rooms, never without a Hale or two (I first came to know the heroic Preston when it was possible to put your cricket trousers on without first taking off your boots), one could always find a mixture of look-alike Sumo wrestlers (*pace* Keith Freeman) and slender-hipped tyros, all equal in the sight of Les Williamson (by the way, Les Williamson is not an Anglo-French dance team). Weirdos occasionally made an appearance but were received with good-humoured tolerance amid an ambience never without a stream of wit.

As I contemplate the end of a glorious era, I am bound to ask how it was that I was so lucky to have been a beneficiary. The secret shall not die with me. I feel it a duty to pass on to fellow Owenians the discovery I made early on, a perception of the prerequisite for achieving full Owenian fellowship while, mark carefully please, not sacrificing lasting marital bliss. Well, if not bliss, a state of suspended hostility. The discovery was, in a word, the stipulation of an absolute condition in my marriage contract that Saturdays, Sundays and public holidays in the cricket season were to be put aside exclusively for Chandos Avenue. If you do that from the word go, substituting Potters Bar these days for Chandos Avenue, you are off and running.

I remember making the point soon after my wife-to-be lured me, complete with a bottle of Maldano's White Lady cocktail which had set me back 6s 9d, a full week's lunch money, into a darkened house ostensibly to see her collection of rare stamps while her parents were out on a visit (I also remember suffering a near seizure when Mum and Dad returned unexpectedly early and found us *in flagrante delicto* but that is another and more dramatic story;

suffice to say that I did what any decent Owenian would be expected to do in that crisis, namely I leaped out of the window and fled through the garden). I never did get to see the stamps and after over 40 years I am beginning to wonder if there ever were any; I suppose they must have gone the same way as her family's alleged claim to ownership of the North American territory of Labrador which I was told when we were courting was going through the Courts. Such was a heady combination of passionate infatuation and gullibility that I found nothing unlikely in this boast and was only momentarily shaken to find that my intended father-in-law thought that Labrador was an island off the coast of New Zealand. He told me that it was famous for its canine exports.

My wife was fairly acquiescent on the issue of weekends at Chandos Avenue up until the wedding and it was not until our return from honeymoon at the Ritz Plaza Family Hotel in Dawlish (five minutes from the sea if you run like hell) and such formalities as arrangements for joint signatures on the bank account were settled, that cricket was mentioned again. I began at this point to detect a hardening of her attitude. There was a certain frisson of hostility which I deduced from some vague hints like 'I'd divorce you tomorrow if I could think of a way of doing it without making you happy', 'We've been married a month already – where did I go wrong?' and 'If you don't come home on Saturday, don't come home on Sunday'.

Her mother was drafted in as a sort of referee. She was a formidable lady who in another life must have been a traffic warden. Frankly, I thought that she knew which side her daughter's bread was buttered on and she might throw her not inconsiderable weight into the argument on my side. But no, if she had to walk on hot coals, she was going to join (if possible, lead) the war against the common enemy and she pronounced crisply, without spilling a single drop of her Guinness, that the issue was plain for anyone to see – she had always maintained and continued so to do, that her daughter was too good for me. For good measure, she asked me if I'd like a punch up the throat. Now the wife's mother was not a woman noted for the prodigality of her vocabulary; her classical education at an LCC Elementary had been foreshortened following the defection of most of the teaching staff in the interests of their own physical safety. Yet those present still recall with awe the terms in which she couched her pronouncement, as succinct as they were picturesque.

Now I was not especially troubled for I knew that many better and more important men than I had been proffered this didactic advice about their inferiority, including Gerry Jones, Harold Moore and Jim Everton. I mean in relation to their wives, not mine. Possibly even Gigs Gwyther as well. I'm not sure about Preston Hale. Certainly not William Hamilton-Hinds.

Anyway at this point, be warned that the wife will take one of two lines. She will either be militant (and there is none more militant than a militant wife) and go for a shoot-out or possibly even metamorphose from a Mary Poppins into a Lysistrata with a threat of withdrawal of favours. The latter case is of course serious and will give you pause. Nevertheless, you must think of Dame Alice (in the nicest way) and remain respectful and regretful but absolutely firm. Remember the wise old adage about the impermanence of a moment of bliss, etc. . . . Or alternatively she may plead. In that case, perhaps you might give just a little if you can't bear to see a grown woman cry, as I did. Tell her she need not do cricket teas *every* Saturday. It might not hurt to offer to buy her a new hat. Tell her gently that to complain that it's not fair is to rely on a mistaken premise, because contrary to common belief, life is not meant to be fair, as was appreciated by the Eton master who used to put all his children under a tarpaulin and beat it indiscriminately in order to teach them that there was indeed no justice in the world.

And lastly, in euphoric but misplaced feelings of compassion do not be tempted into two common errors that you will bitterly regret later. First, remember never, never to come home and try to tell her about the game. She will not want to know, especially about your own half-ton, four wickets for ten, or any other superb part you played. Then above all, resolve never to invite the wife's brother to make up the numbers if you're a man short. Blood is thicker than gin and tonic so that if he does well, she'll never let you forget it but if he makes a bog of it, she'll never forgive you. Especially if, as happened in my case, he takes a ball in the crotch and damages his prospects.

So, fellow classmate, make your play and stand fast. Your future career as an alumnus is in your own hands. Like me, you can win the battle. Of course, you'll lose the war, but that's inevitable. It is written.

One last request. Please do not let a copy of this article get into the hands of my wife; after all, you never know, that Labrador business might turn out to be true.

6

MENS SANA IN CORPORE SANO AND ALL THAT CODSWALLOP

Curiously, not many of us pay heed to the manner of our going once the final curtain comes down. Yet, as one commentator once observed, the only things certain in life are death and taxes. To which we might add that the only uncertainty is in the paperwork involved. Remember the Englishman, who, while holidaying in France, found himself in a small village queuing to use the lavatory. His turn was slow to arrive and noticing his anxiety, the man behind uttered the immortal words of comfort, *'Courage, monsieur, j'entends le papier.'*

The fact is that in one way or another, while we're waiting we poor mortals all trudge through life with the main preoccupation of maximizing a state of good health and fitness and, by so doing, of postponing the date of our inevitable departure when the bell tolls for the soul to leave the body.

During his lifetime, Australian composer Percy Grainger (*In a Monastery Garden* etc. for readers under 60) was a devotee of the *mens sana* cult and was as noted for a pursuit of physical excellence as he was for his music. He thirsted after the achievement of perfect fitness. He did achieve a remarkable level but in spite of years of endeavour, never succeeded in his one overriding ambition; he lived in an average-sized, four-bedroom, suburban house with a modest garden and it was his dream to throw a cricket ball from the back garden high over the roof of the house and then to race through the kitchen and the hall, denuded of furniture, to hurtle out of the front door in time to catch the ball as it came down. A place in the Great Athletes' Hall of Fame was to be his but, alas, try as he would, he never made it. By the way, Percy was not too popular with the neighbours.

For myself, it was at an early age that I became imbued with a resolve not to grow old gracefully but to fight it every step of the way and I sought from the age of ten to become ever fitter and stronger the better to achieve a state wherein I would die in good health. I don't know why – perhaps it was to compensate for lack of inches. Anyway, even at the age of eight, I had saved the requisite number of wrappers from purchases of Cadbury's milk chocolate bars and sent off for a pair of boxing gloves. They were only made of canvas but never mind, they were boxing gloves. As I had no other object on which to use them to build my muscles, I used the chest of drawers in my bedroom as a punch bag; after it fell to pieces, my father gave me some advice about respecting his furniture and then to emphasise his point gave me a walloping. I then turned to arm-hanging on the branches of our apple tree; when the branches snapped and the apple harvest failed, my mother walloped me. Later, my sister and brothers walloped me on principle.

Nevertheless, by the age of twelve, I was committed to a near-ascetic regime of healthcare, exercise and diet. In the interests of inner health and purification of the system and the fight against pimples, I took large dishes of bran and bile beans with added doses of patent remedies like liver salts and Dr J Collis Browne's Chorodyne (1s 6d small size) on a regular basis. I had few close friends in the classroom; I wonder if this was because I used to carry a few cloves of garlic in my pockets to ward off colds. I was doing quite well and had developed the shoulders of a lad of sixteen; the trouble was that I only had the body of a nine-year-old to go with it. However, it was at this stage that I met with a setback. One day in the school gym, I was involved in a miscalculation with the vaulting horse. I took off too soon and my vault was a good foot or so too short to clear the damned animal. As I landed, my entire life passed before me. Tears came to my eyes, I became the possessor of a fine tenor voice and a life of celibacy loomed ahead. These events put a considerable damper on my ambition to become the original Arnold Schwarzenegger, he of the rippling biceps, not helped when I went to the doctor and asked him to prescribe a regime for body building. He looked at me for a moment and his reply was short. 'Try Lourdes,' he said.

After this, my campaign towards total fitness and a deferred demise was much moderated. After all, I reasoned, according to Nostradamus the end of the world is just around the corner anyway. And if not, I might be stricken with the dreaded Vanderman's disease to which it is well known that Owen's cricketers are prone, where the main symptoms are difficulty in spotting a red ball in flight and a tendency to get puffed out after a ten-yards run.

The end came just after my twenty-sixth birthday when I was subjected one memorable night to a serious physical assault.

It began quite innocently. I had made the acquaintance of Mick Duffy through a small advertisement placed in the St Pancras Gazette for work as a builder-handyman; he impressed me as a man who was obviously an influential figure in North West London circles.

His ad was unusual. It read, 'Builder/Handyman, no job too small or too far. Interiors stripped and removed. Reasonable. After my work none of my previous clients intends ever again to employ another handyman. Ring Mr Duffy. Gulliver 9785.' He was particularly proud of the inventive skill in the composition of the copy and quite unconscious of the danger that it might prove a serious discouragement to a reader seeking reliable help. It was only later that I came to appreciate the ominous nature of the reference to interiors being stripped and removed. The pledge of no job being too small or too far was clearly directly related to and dependent on the capacity of a foul-smelling ancient ex-Wall's Ice Cream box tricycle which he had rescued from a scrapyard. Later on, I learned that the offensive effluvium which the tricycle gave off and which communicated itself to the collection of tools left in it, resulted from the carriage of horse manure which Mick collected daily and sold to local market gardeners from his box cycle.

I needed some shelves put up and telephoned what turned out to be Mick's lodgings in Camden Town. He turned up unheralded several days after the date he had promised to appear, a slight, cheerful boyo of about thirty with a spring-like jaunty gait, launching each step from the balls of his feet as if about to break into a jig. Everything about him was brown from the perky farmer boy's hat perched cheekily on the back of his head, as if by an afterthought topping an abundance of tousled curly brown hair, down to the large brown boots that creaked with every step he took. In between, he wore a three-piece brown business-type suit of the 1920s, with 24-inch trouser bottoms.

Mick's encyclopaedic knowledge on every subject was astounding. His perception of every kind of problem and his resourcefulness in their solution was, it appeared, a legend in Camden Town. This expertise soon emerged as he began the fitting of the shelves to my walls and a number of minor hiccups arose. One was the absence of brackets. This was swiftly cured. He was back in a half hour with a supply of brackets; I worried a little as I saw that they were not new and looked as if they had been freshly withdrawn from some long-undisturbed place of rest, I feared to guess where.

The shelvings were not finished for some six weeks. A number of interruptions in the work were occasioned by urgent trips to Dublin 'to see sick friends' and 'to attend to some matters connected with family property holdings', and at other times when he was hit by a mystery virus that could only be controlled by a preparation known as Jameson's, available at a local dispensary. Mick was an engaging fellow and was not ungregarious; he admitted that while he was on the work he was not averse to a visit to the local hostelry. It seemed to me that this was like Guy Fawkes admitting that he lights an occasional firework.

He also allowed that he was not a perfectionist. This had already dawned on me because the finished shelves themselves had a distinctly surrealistic look to them mainly due to the fact that they were constructed from an assortment of woods, including pine, oak, chipboard and even a board of walnut that must have gone missing from the sideboard of one of Mick's puzzled clients. I noticed that some of the boards had 'St Pancras Borough Council' inscribed on the back but I forbore to ask the explanation.

I asked him how much I owed him and after pondering for a while, he said, 'How's about £10, sorr?' Now, £10 happened to be roughly equal to the grand total of all my assets at the time. I must have given some sign of distress, not to mention alarm, because he quickly added, huffily, 'Keep your hair on, guv, what about £5?' Outwardly he was supremely and naïvely indifferent to the accumulation of money but this belied a natural shrewdness. No slouch when it came to financial affairs, he was one of the few men I'd ever met who knew without a moment's hesitation whether it was wiser in betting terms to lay odds of 6–5 on a horse rather than 11–10. He had cleverly reckoned in this instance that the client would jump at a 50 per cent reduction whether or not the ultimate demand was fair. He was right. I swiftly parted with £5.

He once sold me a bottle of pale old sherry ('Direct from Barcelona, sorr,' he emphasized). It was certainly 'pale' as might have been expected, after dilution with distilled water. As to 'old', a week might be a long time in politics but it was even longer in Mick's home distillery.

I saw a lot of Mick. It turned out that he was one of a family of 11 brothers and 2 sisters and had left County Cork to try his luck in London. He had been christened Patrick Joseph but it was subsequently discovered that one of his brothers had already been named Patrick Joseph, a fact that his father had forgotten through having been slightly confused in the midst of the celebrations at Mick's christening. When the mistake was discovered, they decided to call him Mick. Duffy Senior said afterwards that he thought the name was familiar but he wasn't sure. Mrs Duffy consulted Father O'Flynn and after referring to his records he ruled that one of Mick's brothers had indeed been christened Patrick Joseph; this was the one now known as Tommy. The name Francis Xavier was rejected because another of the brothers had been so christened; this was the one called Eddie. The situation having been thoroughly debated from all angles, they all agreed that the most satisfactory solution was that the newest Duffy should be called Mick.

He introduced me to his circle of friends who made up the fast set in the nether regions of Kilburn. It was clear that Mick was their guru. He gave me a run-down of each personality. I was impressed to learn that the men were all important figures in the building industry; I must admit that I felt rather out of it in their company because I didn't know one end of a mechanical digger from the other. On the other hand, although I was a novice in the rarefied world in which such property tycoons move, I was dubious; I certainly wouldn't have bought a used shillelagh from any one of them. Mick explained that he himself was a master building contractor but that he filled in with handyman work, 'as a hobby, y'understand'.

Most of the feminine contingent were said by Mick to be well known for their work in public entertainment; I decided that this meant that they were professional performers of some kind, probably theatrical. I think I heard him mutter the word 'strippers' and supposed that they helped Mick and his colleagues with stripping work in their spare time. They all seemed nice, a bright chatty bunch who immediately took me to their bosoms, which, I could not help observing, were generally speaking admirably and amply suited and displayed for the purpose.

It was at a private party one Saturday night, held in a small flat in the basement of a large cavernous Victorian house off the Kentish Town Road, that Mick introduced me to a young lady. 'She's a princess, the hottest thing in town, sorr,' he whispered.'If you're a friend of Mick Duffy's, you're a friend of mine,' she proclaimed. I must draw a veil over the astonishing speed and warmth of the progression of our friendship assisted by the proximity of several cases of stout and Babycham, but soon realized as never before what a dazzlingly romantic, witty and seductive person I must be, and it was not long before I found myself alone with her in a small bare bedsitter on an upper floor of the house. We sat on the bed and although she seemed far from relaxed, I put it down to the likelihood that she was nervous and of a shy disposition. She told me of her background. Her family had extensive land interests in Ireland and she herself had been educated at a convent and subsequently, she said, had graduated at the University of Killarney. I was surprised at this because I had never heard of the latter academic establishment and it only served to remind me that my interests and preoccupations up to then had been far too sheltered. Brenda, for that was her name, had come to London to visit the many members of her family who had settled in Camden Town (I found this highly credible) and was working as an international model under the professional name of Fiona LaTouche at the Galtymore Academy of Art in Kilburn High Road. She added that the school was under the patronage of members of the Royal Family but that she had been told to be discreet when asked which royals were involved.

I grew rapidly more interested in her. She was blonde, 5 feet 8 inches, very full of figure. She was clad in a flimsy creation that was both striking and modest, striking because it was of an imitation leopard skin material, soft to touch, and modest because it had been cut with masterly economy, low at the top and short with a tiny slit skirt. When I say low at the top I mean that it could be described as an off-the-shoulder frock, although in fact it was not so much off-the-shoulder as off-the-chest. To put it at its highest, it could only be described as scanty and did not pretend to cover anything important. She wore a number of baubles around her neck and arms, was heavily perfumed and her face was generously made-up, lavishly mascaraed and rouged. To me it all appeared over-showy but then I remembered what Mick had told me and I realized that it befitted Fiona's status as a theatrical star. One had to bear in mind that as Mick had said, she was in a professional class of her own and was sitting on a gold mine!

By now I was becoming confused by an urgency which had begun to surge in my loins. My comfortable home and in-bed-by-ten routine had never contemplated such a situation. On the one hand, I'd had little first-hand experience of women and even less of sex and I agonized on the best way to proceed. On the other, unused through my training to a heavy alcohol intake, the consumption of two or three pints of stout and Babycham (Mick assured me that, 'It has to be good for you, sorr, it's the Pope's favourite drink, God bless and save him.') followed by chasers of extra-strong lager and cider 'snakebites', of which I had only a hazy recollection, were rendering me nauseous; what I wanted above all was to be violently sick.

I focused my mind on the central issue which was whether to try to progress the affair with a bold approach or alternatively, to be sick into the sink. However, my jaw must have dropped at least three inches as the situation changed and suddenly became ugly. I haven't mentioned that she spoke with a thick Irish brogue and it is true that I had some difficulty in following much of what she said;

I may therefore have missed some warning that she uttered but the abrupt change in her was nevertheless startling. To say that I was shocked would be a gross understatement. I could not imagine what I had done to upset her. I mean it's absurd, as if I could really get anyone into Hollywood movies! Surely the silly girl hadn't taken me seriously. In any case, the mask of sensuality fell away and she was suddenly eyeing me with an expression that unmistakably threatened grievous bodily harm. I think I heard her murmur something about my needing discipline.

She rose quickly and locked the door. She returned and began unceremoniously to remove my clothing item by item while at the same time discarding her own. I was particularly shaken at this because I was wearing a handsome Savile Row-type blue velvet smoking jacket; it hadn't actually come from Savile Row for I had bought it new at the Fifty Shilling Tailors that very morning. With blue suede Cuban-heeled shoes it made up an ensemble of which I was particularly proud; I noticed that it had excited a good deal of admiration and envy at the party. [Frankly, I had not been greatly impressed with the style of the garments worn by the others there; there was a great deal of green but it seemed to me that the emphasis generally was workaday and far from svelte.]

Undeterred, Fiona continued the energetic process of relieving me of my sartorial elegance and the other items of clothing down to, and including, my special thermal underwear, all except my socks. I learned from an expert later on that for some reason it was the done thing to leave the socks on. She deftly dropped away her own clothes and stood for a moment *au naturel*. I looked away; I have always tried to do the decent thing. I have to admit that I was somewhat deflated as I caught sight of myself in the door mirror; the image of great dignity I had hoped I was presenting was dented by the revelation of a protruding big toe of comic proportions through a large hole in the left member of the thick warm army socks lovingly hand-knitted by my Auntie Maude. When I turned back (I have to confess, fairly soon) she had donned a very short nightie, a wisp of a garment sweetly beribboned at the chest. She explained that she wore it in case of a fire.

At any rate, as farce transmuted into Grand Guignol the mask of sensuality fell away in an instant and was replaced by a virtuoso exhibition of quite incredible ferocity. The sublime dramatically became ridiculous. I could not imagine what I had done to upset her. Discretion is the better part of valour, better to be sensible here than heroic, I told myself. In any case, I rationalized, the scenario was becoming quite intriguing. But she then unleashed a ferocious attack and started to whack me with what appeared to be a carpet-beater. My head was swimming and although I affected to laugh nervously, I rose smartly and cowered at the other side of the bed. She seemed put out by my efforts to dodge the blows and produced from a cupboard a whip and various other instruments with which she lost no time in belabouring me. I skipped and stumbled round the room with her in full pursuit, but there was no escaping and she caught me again and again across the buttocks with the butt of the whip. 'Come here, ye sleepy bugger,' she shrieked between blows. She seemed quite annoyed. I was sweating. Protesting, I sank exhaustedly back on to the bed. I wondered briefly why she pinned me down and was apparently bent on taking my inside leg measurement but I forgot that riddle when she selected from the cupboard a cane and, for God's sake, proceeded to give me six of the best. Then she took up the whip and devoted herself to giving me a damn good hiding. And for no reason at all that I could think of.

By this time, the intoxicating smell of the cheap musky Nights of Old Baghdad perfume that filled the room, the nausea, the drink and the thrashing I was getting were combining to dull my consciousness, and at this point I passed out. I came to to find that the situation had taken another extraordinary turn; Fiona stood over me, now dressed in school uniform complete with gym slip, black stockings and suspenders. As she moved I saw that the uniform was completely backless. Was this some strange new cult? I leaped up but it was a mistake. With an Irish whip followed by a double-folding back press, she had me on the canvas again. She went to the cupboard and came back quickly with some heavy chains. Helplessly pinned down, I realized now that my struggle to defend myself was to be of no avail. I felt a sense of inevitability; I was too weak to protest. I simply could not understand the metamorphosis of a sweet well-bred girl of fine family into a psychopath with homicidal intent, but it was too much; my will to resist crumbled and I resolved not to resist but to humour her. The order of the day must be Lie Back and Think of England. I did not report her but left quietly and painfully the following morning.

As I hobbled rather than walked home, I was surprised to find that I was whistling a tune. The tune was *Ain't Misbehaving*. Looking back, I felt that I had learned much from what had been an epic affair. Above all, it had opened my eyes to a fact which was not publicly known, namely the amazing range and excellence of the curriculum offered to its lucky pupils by a convent education. All-in wrestling yet as well! Something else was nagging away at the back of my head but I couldn't quite pin it down. It wouldn't drop into place but I remembered what it was as I lay in bed that night, running for the umpteenth time through the events of the night before; it was that I must go to Jones Brothers and get myself a new pair of socks. The smart lads were wearing patterned socks with clocks, weren't they? And while there, ask if they do leather gear.

However, strangely, this vicious attack opened a new vista and my dedication to a spartan regime with cold showers suddenly seemed overdone. Up to now there had been no room for women or other deviations in my programme for fitness of body and mind, but I reconsidered.

Next day, I dumped the exercise bike along with the clean-living charts. It occurred to me that there might be more to life than a gruelling quest for physical perfection and I thought I would try the fast lane for a while. By which I mean that among other changes of lifestyle, the abstemious and frugal regimen was discarded; instead of a joint and two veg a typically balanced dinner menu now involved enough cholesterol to kill a half-dozen American businessmen. Often seen in the company of a blonde, about 5 feet 8 inches, very full of figure, I was soon the envy of the deprived iron-pumping brigade.

But there was still the question how best to order the manner of my going. To some of us the competence still to direct the passage of events after our role here is ended is extraordinarily attractive. The subject of one's ashes and the rights of a citizen in their disposition is currently much in the public eye. Actor Trevor Howard's wish that his remains be scattered on the square at Lord's has recently been denied by the authorities there. An Australian entrepreneur has offered Mick Jagger a vast sum for his ashes, hoping eventually to sell them in hourglasses for hundreds of thousands of pounds each. Not for a song, obviously. When Dorothy Parker, star of literary New York in the twenties, died in 1967, her ashes ended up in a filing cabinet in her accountant's office while the question of their disposal was being debated; his public-spirited proposal that they be split into little packages for sale to the many Parker admirers was seriously considered but happily, since last year, they have taken up permanent residence in a memorial garden. Other bizarre stories have lately been reported including that of a lady whose husband went missing after a hostess refused to let his ashes go onto a flight with luggage destined for Boston, Massachusetts. She has lodged a law suit for $75,000. She reluctantly had to agree that the claim could not include damages for the loss of conjugal enjoyment.

This public ventilation has motivated me to reconsider

my original intentions and I have decided that on the whole it would be unwise to hold to my plan for the dispersal of my ashes over the cricket pitch of my old club of such happy memories for two reasons. Firstly, there must be a distinct and alarming possibility of miscalculation on the part of the contractors entrusted with the job (especially if they engage some cowboy out of the local paper to do it). Let's face it, I'm not all that big and my ashes will likely not be terribly heavy, so that it wouldn't take much in the way of an air eddy or a sudden change of wind to find my remains floating gently down on to, say, the Tottenham Hotspurs F C ground or even, God forbid, Chelsea. Death is pretty final but I don't fancy them being trampled on by a mob of football ruffians singing, *Wish me Luck as you Wave me Goodbye*. Secondly, even if a safe landing is achieved, there might be a question mark over one's chances of resting in peace; some of the lads get very boisterous after the match, when they've supped a few on a Saturday night.

I would certainly stipulate that the scattering ceremony should take place only if the weather is calm with clear visibility. But even then, I am mindful of the tale of the chap who turned out wearing his best brand new camel-hair coat at the scattering of his cricketer father's ashes at the Kennington Oval, one wintry day in March. The coat was a smart deep-pleated affair. In the interests of cutting costs, the funeral director dispensed with an urn and delivered the ashes in a large Sainsbury's pickles jar (the deceased was a big man). The formalities over, just as the jar was unscrewed, a stiff wind blew up and all the ashes blew back into the deep pleats and folds of the chap's new coat where they lodged and stuck. The coat had to go to the cleaners. That is how father's ashes finished up in the back room of the Brixton branch of Sketchley's Dyers and Cleaners where, so far as we know, they still repose, unhonoured and unsung.

No, if my ashes are to be dispersed according to my direction, it would effectively represent my last earthly wish and I reckon therefore that I'm entitled to a little self-indulgence. *Ex hypothesi*, after profound consideration, I think I'd like them scattered in the Can-Can dancers' dressing-room at the Folies Bergere.

I only hope my ashes will be up to it. I mustn't lose face on the other side.

7

ASPECTS OF THE WAY WE WERE or THE AMAZING AFFAIR OF THE BEADLE'S PIE

In a world troubled with a myriad of problems, to let the memory wander nostalgically down the years to our own school-days must be the second-best thing to do on a rainy afternoon. With all the current talk about the exposure of children to the toxic foodstuffs, drugs, drink and the rest, and the dangerous habits that young people pick up, one can't help wondering if we suffered so seriously at Owen's in the twenties and thirties, a pre-Benidorm time when getting a man into space was but a dream and you could get a reply from Directory Enquiries. What did we get up to? How did we overcome?

The first test was school dinners. There was no coddling for us there. John Turner certainly didn't get his habit of a touch of *paté de foie gras* or a spoonful of caviare with his preprandial vodka from school dinners. Nor was Ken Attrill's insistence that his lobster be kissed with truffles in cognac born in the Owen's dining hall. Preston Hale's penchant for *feuilleté* of wild strawberries with sour cream, followed by *cafe viennoise* and petits fours, is well known at Le Gavroche, but it was not a taste developed in Owen Street.

School dinners were no less than epic. Seated in the bare tiled basement at Owen Street amid the hubbub and chatter of a hundred or more young savages with monstrous appetites, vast quantities of food were consumed, food which our latter-day nutrition experts would have condemned out of hand as dangerous to health. The main course would feature orthodox roast beef, deep-fried fish cakes or plump sausages, with chips or mash, garnished with greased bubble and squeak or mushy peas. Sometimes, however, it would be pie à la Deeley. Deeley was the importantly uniformed beadle who, with his wife, supervised the kitchen and the dining arrangements and, against all the odds, managed to stay sane. They were both said to be highly qualified for their job, by which we could only assume that they had City and Guilds certificates in plumbing. The extraordinary pie was their masterpiece but was a concoction to which such savants as Harold Moore gave a name as would shock the gentle readers of this essay if it were to appear in print. There was much speculation as to what unnatural ingredients went into Deeley's pie and concern that it carried no government health warning; only comprehensive dowsing in tomato ketchup neutralized its worst effects. One report had it that anti-vivisectionists evinced a deal of curiosity about it. But nobody ever succeeded in lifting the protective curtain of secrecy the beadle had drawn around his arcane mixture. Under interrogation he maintained a courteous but impenetrable silence and took his secret with him to the grave.

There followed the jewel in the crown, the pudding. It would be spotted dick, suet pudding or rhubarb crumble, all chock-full of sugar and fat, topped with lumpy custard. Health-threatening maybe, but scrumptious basic fodder for growing lads. And not bad for a shilling, all inclusive.

Uncaring of the lethal implications of this intake, we would compound the damage by stuffing ourselves with sausage rolls, bags of Smith's crisps, chocolate whirls and slabs of Cadbury's fruit and nut, from the tuck shop in the corner of the playground, kept by the avuncular Collins of the flowing moustaches, or if at the Field that afternoon, from dear Mrs Coleman's window. If still not replete, it would sometimes be spaghetti on toast at Lyons if pocket money permitted; what a good thing McDonald's hadn't come on the scene yet. In my own case, I shudder to recall that my mother worried that I wasn't eating enough and fed me bowls of chicken soup with dumplings every day as part of a build-up supplement. I became distinctly portly. Some would have said fat. And did.

Health regulations were lax, fridges and iceboxes scarce, yet so far as I remember, we heard little of salmonella, listeria, toxic bread, cattle madness and sundry other bacterial dangers that are everyday topics today. The dangers of consuming lightly cooked eggs, ripe cheese, chicken, chilled meals and heaven knows what else, stigmatized as heinous today, were not in issue. The Islington Gazette carried no reports of the incidence of incipient cryptosporidiosis from drinking tap water. Today, it is hot news. I even read this week that a London doctor has found a recipe for removing the 'gas' from baked beans. I hope he isn't serious; it would take all the fun out of it.

Evidently, according to the pundits' scientific rules we were killing ourselves by eating all the wrong foods. Paraphrasing Jackie Mason, Owen's must have been the only place the world where eating was more dangerous than sex.

Secondly, there was no drug taking, no drunkenness (at any rate, by the pupils; Manual Smith and one or two other members of the staff took an occasional glass – for medicinal purposes only, they swore), and there was little smoking. There were also no serious signs of bad language. In the face of a violent and unscripted explosion that wrecked a part of the lab, Armitage (Chemistry) merely called me an ass, a twit and a dummy. Indeed, I was hurt and disappointed when in one of Jimmy Cracknell's French lessons, which had descended as usual into a state of pandemonium, (in which descent I regret to have to confess that I was a prominent participant),

Cracknell of the sallow countenance, after staring at me as if I had made a bad smell, then called into question the marital state of my parents. And he prefaced this egregious observation with a reference to my lack of height, using a hyphenated expression of which the first part was 'short'. I believe in fact that in the common room afterwards, his proposition was supported by the choleric Ben Morgan. The irony was that both of these men were themselves short-arsed but perhaps that is beside the point. The important element was that they were both wrong; although they were not well up in irregular French verbs, my parents were pillars of Tufnell Park respectability.

I ought to add that baiting the teaching staff, poor devils, was kept to a reasonable level. A stink bomb or two, a little chalk in Jock Rees's ink-well to cause the ink to froth up on to the ceiling, or the reversal of the drawer sections of his desk to test the good man's reactions, could surely not be termed excessively mischievous. It was entirely untrue that after one particularly cruel fifth form session Jock was found whimpering on a narrow ledge outside his window. The unbuttoning of 'Soapy' Grant's braces when the lights were lowered in the course of a physics experiment could scarcely be labelled seriously delinquent; after all, his trousers stayed up. We were fair about it and both warring sides seemed to accept the situation with grace and good humour. Loud belching from the back of the classroom (Peter Lawler) while Jesse Smith's back was turned had to be seen as more unsocial than wayward. And there was no truth at all in the rumour that Mr Hutchings needed a police escort for admission to his own fourth form classroom. Certainly Ernie Bowyer continued to make plain his affection for his pupils.

The rapport was soured somewhat, it is true, when Head Master Asman committed a gaffe in regard to a boy named Hakim. Hakim was Persian and had originally come from the province of his country which shared a common border with Turkey. Asman remembered that this was the case and that he was either a Turk or a Kurd but, try as he would, he could not recall which. It was unfortunate that he became confused and decided in school assembly to compromise by calling Hakim neither a Turk nor a Kurd but took the middle course and in describing Hakim's race used a word which was an amalgam of Turk and Kurd. Hakim took it personally and was naturally displeased, it is said by those who were seated near him that he made a response that consisted of two non-Persian words only. And they weren't 'Merry Christmas'.

Thirdly, there was sex. It did not play a serious part in our agenda. We knew that men and women were different but we weren't too sure quite how. For myself, my notions about the physiognomy of the opposite sex were naïve and tentative until I left school. No one had explained. My secret thoughts were in fact much occupied with a pretty, fresh-faced, curly-haired boy for a while until I went to a party when I was sixteen and met an Owen's girl who was as shy and introverted as I was. She was extremely plain and with long hair decorated with a pink bow looked from the back like the winning dog at Cruft's. Unfortunately, from the front she looked like the losing dog. But she was eager to learn and, as you would expect from an Owen's girl, full of bright ideas. She did much to advance my education.

Meanwhile, with an inchoate soft porn industry, we satisfied ourselves with harmless diversions of the sniggering tee-hee-hee variety, like surreptitious reading in class of *Lady Chatterley's Lover* (unexpurgated), *The Well of Loneliness* (which I understood not at all but at which I affected worldly amusement), *Kama Sutra* and other works of less literary merit but greater crudity.

Press accounts of prurient public scandals like the sexual perambulations of the infamous Rector of Stiffkey in Norfolk with nubile young girls, and of Colonel Barker, the transvestite army officer, were devoured avidly and made the base of weak sex-orientated jokes and limericks. Reverend Davidson's exposure ended with his defrocking and exhibition in a cage in Blackpool, good material for dissemination of a further bout of scatological graffiti on the lavatory walls, where I recall that the inscriptions were generally more subtle than crude. I remember one which went 'Oedipus, please ring your mother at once'. Near the knuckle double entendres from the likes of Max Miller at the Islington Empire or Collins' Music Hall we thought the height of daring and were convulsed. I was fascinated and excited when at one first house performance at the Finsbury Park Empire, Gracie Fields's bra strap snapped under the strain of reaching for a very high note and revealed for all to see a small left breast, resembling a spaniel's ear, naked under her diaphanous gown. I bored the chaps for some days with this, to me, major item. Even an organized school visit (I think it was to the National Gallery) to see Botticelli's *Birth of Venus* excited much interest when the first contingent reported back that she was totally unclothed. It was all so innocent in retrospect. It is so true, innocence is a wonderful thing, what a shame to waste it on children.

Television hadn't arrived so sex and violence in the media had no display vehicle; our viewing was confined to visits to the local movie palace to lick our lips over such 'hot' numbers as Clara Bow and Jean Harlow. In deference to warnings about the danger of going blind or getting a crooked back, most of us eschewed personal indulgences. In general, our reading was of the *Magnet* and *Gem*. Typical gestures of our independence and macho daring were off-limits visits (sometimes in lesson time) to the Goswell Road Snooker Hall and furtive forays to the back room of the Crown and Woolpack. My fellow renegades were Doug Young, Laurie Ambler and Louis Pinto, not giant academics but great characters. There was no bullying or in-house scandal. We, the rabble, expended our surplus energies in noisy clashes in the playground while the academic virtuosi headed by

Hicks, Harrison and Creamer, brilliant wranglers, went off elsewhere to propound theorems to each other. Thus it was that in our different ways we mopped up some of the pie syndrome and the cholesterol excesses that we must have ingested.

These were the pleasant days of wine and roses at Islington. Nothing was there to portend a bad end for us and I don't know of any who became murderers, rapists or bank robbers. On the contrary, I do know of many who have a proud record of excellence and service in the community and could be trusted to fight each other's corner when need arose, especially for Owen's or Owenians. The aim of schooling nowadays is said to be, 'to prepare pupils for an informed and active involvement in family, social and civic life'; Owen's did that for us.

So, sere and yellow now, we can take pride that as emergent citizens we walked the moderate line. But, you will ask, what of Deeley's pie that played such an important role in our formative years? What devilish formula had he stumbled on? We can only speculate. Certainly he did not spare himself in his experiments on dysenteric warfare behind locked doors of his kitchen lab. That he was a patriot is unchallengeable. It is said that in World War II when our fortunes were at a low ebb, our people were astute enough to drop large quantities of the pie, disguised in Walls' packets, behind the enemy lines, a move that saved our bacon and is estimated moreover to have shortened the War by at least a year. Intelligence had revealed that facilities in Occupied France were woefully antiquated and inadequate in number and the terrible Beadle's Pie Drop took swift and devastating toll of the Boche. It soon became evident that the enemy had sustained hundreds of thousands of casualties in the wake of this stratagem. Reports filtered through that some crack troops actually blew up in action. One brigade commander was captured in a corner of a field, helpless with his breeches around his ankles; that was one corner of a foreign field that would forever be German. Enterologists were conscripted and sent to the front from all over Europe but to no avail; they were impotent to counter the deadly pie. They had no supplies of penicillin or tomato ketchup. We remember the exultant headline in the London *Times*, trumpeting, 'Deeley Pie Drop Has Jerry On The Run'.

In his war memoirs, Winston Churchill paid tribute to the beadle and the debt the nation owed to Deeley's Pie, arguably, he wrote, the most important secret weapon since the advent of the haggis.

For ourselves, we may well be proud that we were the guinea-pigs. A wrecked digestive system is a small price to pay. It's sad but when all is said and done you cannot beat McHugh's Law which warns that in all human endeavour the odds are never better than 11 to 8 against. So, alas, it's steamed fish, boiled rice, dry crackers and alka seltzer for supper; the heartburn is hell at three o'clock in the morning.

8

MAYONNAISE IS IN THE EYE OF THE BEHOLDER

It was in another essay that I wrote that there is no mention of murderers, rapists or bank robbers in the chronicles of famous ex-scholars of my *alma mater*. By extension one is proud and relieved to report that after a combination of the training, self-discipline and osmosis received in their time at school, the alumni are noted for their principled attitudes, dependability and pragmatism. The fellers and the girls are realistic in social outlook and tend to live out life as they find it, not as they would have wished it to be.

What led me to these agreeable conclusions was my ruminating the other day on the kind of image we present. Admittedly we are properly dedicated to the time-honoured triumvirate of wine, women and song. First, on wine, I do not claim that we are oenophiles or that sundowners on the terraces of Potters Bar are *kir royales*, but I promise you I would unhesitatingly bet the wife's secret nest-egg on one of my brethren in a brew-tasting contest. Second, as for women, their fastidious choice needs no further or better evidence than a look at their ladies. And substituting men for women, the girls certainly don't drag their dainty feet either, if the tales told in the bar are half accurate. Which leaves us with the third of the trio, song. Well, I have to admit that we don't seem to boast a surfeit of Pavarottis but don't be surprised to read soon of our up-and-coming stars.

It follows that for myself, I owe allegiance to this shrine of the moderate, the pragmatic and the provable rather than the tendentious or the emotional; I have no desire to further obfuscate a philosophy that is already labyrinthine with weird theories. I believe in what I can actually see. But I acknowledge that the numbers of those who seek understanding and solutions through that which they cannot plainly see, are many. I cannot accept that the wearing of a metal pyramid on your forehead can bring up your vibrations and promote peace in the world. On the other hand, for example, my wife is taken with the powers of the supernormal and is receptive to hidden significances and symbolism. She relates readily to magnetic influences and meaningful signs. I am a sceptic; I remember that a certain editor once told me that every time he refers to a psychic journal and gets a name wrong, he has a phone call the next day, complaining. He asks, quite fairly, why if the journal in question had been genuinely into premonitions, did they not ring up the day before.

For instance, my wife is convinced that if you suffer with leg cramps in the night you should put a cork in the bed, or if you want to find something you've mislaid, turn a glass upside down. Trouble is she can't remember which is which. The other night, having mislaid her house keys, she slept with a cork under the sheets. The result was that not only were her keys still missing but in the morning the cork was also found to have vanished; there have been various guesses as to the fate of the cork, ranging from the bizarre to the unthinkable. She has now decided, by a process of elimination, to try the upturned glass ploy to see if she could locate the cork. The only news to date is that the cork, the keys and now the glass are all missing. However, the good news is that she has rid herself of the leg cramps; these have now been transferred to me.

NEWSFLASH: I mislaid my favourite suede driving gloves yesterday. With great acuity my wife at once stood a glass tumbler upside down where it would catch the eye of the great lost and found registrars in the sky. This morning she announced with a triumphant I-told-you-so air that the gloves had come to light in a stair cupboard. I put them on humbly and gratefully. I found both to be left-handed gloves. Make of that what you will.

When I quoted Pliny the Elder, a fairly sensible old cove, as opining sagely that to inquire what is beyond is no concern of man nor can the human mind form any conjecture concerning it, the wife said she doesn't trust Neapolitans and in any case she's felt for some time that old Pliny is past his prime and is due for the funny farm. She is firmly of the belief that when we leave this earthly state, we progress to another plane for reincarnation. She claims that she has had proof that her existential theory has actually befallen her mother and father, my late in-laws. She avers that she has had irrefutable signs that a pair of birds, one a gull and the other a pigeon, to be found in the Southern Californian resort of La Corona, are respectively her father and mother, reborn. Accordingly, we now make regular annual pilgrimages to La Corona to an hotel from whose balcony there are commanding views of the ocean. Other less enlightened mourners only have to journey to the resting places of their dear departed in Streatham or Golders Green; my cross is to travel 10,000 miles to commune, grey with jetlag, with a pair of birds.

On the last visit, the assault by my in-laws, together with an army of other gulls and sea pigeons, as they invaded the balcony, perching on the railings or descending to the terrace itself, fluttering wildly and squawking for scraps, the while shedding droppings and turning the balcony into a gigantic birds' mess, was unnerving, to put it mildly. We were up to our bongos in detritus. With the scrimmage for the day's menu, it is clear that there is nothing in the gulls' manual about there being no such thing as a free lunch. Yet the wife decrees that the journey halfway round the world must be undertaken not only out of filial respect but so as to ensure that they are nourished with some decent rations. It was only with great difficulty that I dissuaded her from taking a Fortnum's hamper with potted shrimps, lamb cutlets and blancmange – I only got my way when I pointed out that the birds were starting to look a little obese.

I ought to explain that my late father-in-law was a fish and poultry caterer, an honourable trade and when you come to think about it probably the oldest profession, older than those that claim that distinction. And less punishing. I recall that when he consented to giving his daughter's hand, and anything else I thought might be useful, to me in marriage during the War when there was a shortage of luxury foodstuffs, he promised me a dowry in the shape of a side of smoked salmon. Now Bob had several special interests, principal among which were four – an unquenchable search for fast horses, an insatiable ambition to bankrupt the entire British bookmaking fraternity, a formidable thirst for brandy and an inordinate smoking habit. In the event, the date of our wedding came just after Ascot and inconvenienced Bob, finding him with a slight cash flow problem; the bookies, he stated, had temporary custody of his funds. (He couldn't be blamed for being unprepared; I'd only been courting his daughter for eight years.) However, he argued not unreasonably that he could not let such incidentals as his daughter's dowry eat into his last reserves. Bob was above all consistent; he always followed the principle that his financial programme must not be hampered by considerations of morals or ethics. Thus, while the fair hand etc. of his daughter materialized at the due date, the side of salmon did not. What is more, I was landed with the bill for the wedding reception. My wife tried to make up for the absence of the salmon by feeding me tinned salmon rissoles for supper every night for 16 weeks. It got so that I started getting an urge to dive into the river and leap upstream. I had to caution her about the offence of salmon abuse before she desisted.

I would not dare openly to doubt my wife's beliefs, mainly because I don't wish to suffer some terrible punishment like deprivation of the traditional and inalienable Sunday morning right of every Englishman (for details, see end of this piece), but I have to admit that I would only believe that the seagull is my father-in-law if it flew in with a side of salmon under one wing, a copy of *Sporting Life* under the other, a barrel of brandy around its neck and a fag drooping from its beak. For one thing, the gull just does not look like a born-again fish caterer. With his beady eyes and sharp features he looks more like an accountant with a tricky VAT problem. *Au contraire*, my late father-in-law was a tall handsome man with dark dramatic features, a sort of Holloway Road Rudolph Valentino. The gull is thickset with a hint of a beer gut, tight-assed and not at all sexy.

There were many tales of Bob's exploits in World War I, of how he was regimental heavyweight champion, how he was bitten by a snake in Africa (I personally thought this a load of cobras) and how after a long spell in the trenches he became bored, so bored that he was even prepared to go back home to his wife, so he shot himself in the foot. Headquarters had begun to realize that Bob's activities could seriously impede the Allied war effort and his medical discharge was arranged swiftly. (Memo: *Take a look at the gull's pedal extremities and see if he's foot perfect.*) This was a man deeply respected and even hallowed by the venerable burghers of Islington, a man who had downed a yard of ale in a pub in Upper Street in under 42 seconds. It is said that when his funeral cortège passed the Dog and Duck, the crowds lining the streets even outnumbered those who greeted the victorious Arsenal Cup team. One prominent mourner was the manager of the bank where Bob had taken a personal loan on ten years repayment terms when he'd been told that he had only six weeks to live. Another, quite inconsolable, was from the Bookmakers' Protection Society.

To be fair, the bird did evince one or two signs of a

possible connection. One evening, I left a gin and tonic on the terrace. On my return, it had gone. Perched on the rail, with an impish smirk on his face and his beak mockingly open, he looked me straight in the eye with all the sincerity of a time-share tout. His consort, the handsome full-bosomed pigeon, who in certain respects resembled Elizabeth Taylor (I think the respects are called 44DD), was perched nearby and I'm sure I heard her choked caw to her mate, 'Gelt up, Gog' (pigeonspeak for 'Belt up, Bob'). Then she pouted, sniffed, preened herself and strutted away so importantly you'd have thought she'd invented the wheel. Bob followed her but left me a present on the terrace table which I regret to report I absent-mindedly tried to brush off, thinking that it was mayonnaise.

He'd always been a staunch Arsenal supporter. One day, I caught him on the wing, scanning the London paper. When he saw they'd lost 2–1 at Tottenham, he took off furiously and dumped the paper in the sewage pit. Not absolute proof but, perhaps, circumstantial evidence.

But I still don't believe in the supernormal. I suspect that many of the unexplained happenings reported in the media can be ascribed to nearby electronic garage door openers. However, I keep an open mind on the question of another life after this one. Indeed, like Sir Arthur Conan Doyle, I am willing in the interests of theosophical science to attempt contact from the other side in some prearranged way. Regrettably, Sir Arthur's pre-terminal compact has failed. I am prepared to settle the issue finally by initiating from the other side a positive and conclusive test to determine if there is a channel for communicating. For example, I would undertake on a given Saturday afternoon at 4 p.m. GMT precisely, to transfer two of the pebbles from the coat pocket of the umpire at the bowler's end to that of the square leg umpire in whatever 1st XI match is taking place at Cooper's Lane, so that the former finds that he has only four pebbles and the latter has eight. At the same instant, the ball will disappear and will be found together with a bag of sawdust in the kitchen of the Han Wong Chinese Takeaway in Finchley High Road. The bag of sawdust will be clearly marked to prevent confusion with the dish of the day.

If all this works, I hope we can agree that we have adduced indisputable evidence of life after death, a thesis which has incidentally long been advanced with exceeding rudeness by some who have noted my continued appearance on the cricket field.

Meanwhile, I've learned one useful lesson from the great seagull debate. If I come back, it will not be as a bird; it'll be as a bookie.

LATE NEWS: The riddle of the birds may have been resolved. This morning we found a mess of bloodied feathers scattered about the balcony. Something awful had occurred. Has it all ended with the demise of the grande dame *pigeon? Are we looking at foul play, a case of wife battering? And the seagull hasn't appeared today and is thought to be on the run. He's been seen at a racetrack bar, crying, drunk and broke. Watch this space.*

Footnote: An Englishman's traditional and inalienable Sunday morning right = breakfast in bed.

9

OUR PART IN THE HISTORY OF THE WORLD OR ARE YOU SITTING COMFORTABLY?

If anyone you know happens to suggest that the part played by Owenians in world affairs in the past quadrennium has been jejune, you may well be indignant. The truth is that contemporary historical scholarship will be ill-served if it is not seen that only a becoming sense of modesty and a commendable disdain for self-advertisement have kept from the public eye the predominance of this ancient and respected educational establishment over many less modest and more vaunted institutions such as Eton, Harrow, *et al*.

In 600 years time, when we shall all be no more (except, I suspect, indestructibles like *Coronation Street* [and the wife's mother]), it will be millennium time for Owen's School and some clever dick will dig up these essays as a record of our lifestyle and the way we were in a bygone era when scheduled hourly services of interplanetary communion with Mars were unheard of and travellers to Majorca were first locked up at Gatwick for nine hours at a time, when you had to pump fuel into a car before it would go, when swimming the Atlantic was thought impossible, and interest rates on credit cards were only 38.4%. As you know, I have also written under the name of Edmund Burke and have a reputation as an essayist as well as a Burke. It is therefore my duty to compile these modest pieces to adduce evidence of the Owen's contribution in an evolving civilization. Modest indeed when placed next to such masterly works as RA Dare's *History of the School* but then Dare was a fine historian, a teacher *sans pareil* and an exceptionally great and good man.

We don't want the essays to come to light prematurely. I'll hide them behind the bar at our clubhouse in a tin marked Cocoa. That'll ensure that they don't come to light for at least 600 years, if ever.

Various notable incursions into world affairs obtrude themselves on my memory. For instance, was it not an Owenian, a certain Waldo Tobias, who in the year 1693 finally laid to rest the thesis that the world was flat. Some scientists were theorizing that if the world were round the water in our bath would be much higher in the middle than at either end; Waldo, famed for his work in IIIA and later at Neasden University on underwater eruptions and gas secretions in bath water, pointed out that they had overlooked the sucking force (I think I've got that right) of Australian water consumption down under which had an exactly opposite and levelling influence. This learned contribution to international hydroscientific knowledge has been ranked alongside Newton's Second Law of Thermodynamics in world importance, and is now known as Tobias's Leak. It is believed that one of Waldo's descendants has recently distinguished himself at Owen's with ideas of similar profundity.

Among so many, another instance of Owenian resource lay behind the evolution of basic domestic building and sanitary development; it was the three-seater toilet. Archaeologists have recently uncovered such an artefact in a dig at Highbury Corner and have wondered at its origins. I can disclose that this remarkable technical structure came from the labours and the drawing-board of two eighteenth century Os, Paulinus and Kenith Rowsbury, who lived in the little hamlet of Tufnell Parc. Having left school with but one 'O' level in woodwork and having failed the entry exam for the YTS, the two youths soon became known for their enterprise with wood and pottery. They were shrewd and versatile and although we have not actually found evidence of it, were probably also skilled drovers, because the records sometimes refer to them as the Rowsbury cowboys.

There are amazing tales of what and whom they knocked up in the back room of their little MFI workshop. Encouraged by the successful debut of an air-conditioned hamster cage, they hit on the idea of a three-seater toilet, a concept to open doors of convenience to the public previously undreamed of. They worked for years on perfecting the idea and although Paulinus's patience flagged at times and he became weary, Kenith spurred him on with the assurance that they would be rich one day. 'We are sitting on a fortune,' he would tell Paulinus. Readers who, like Paulinus and Kenith, are familiar with French habits through their subscription to academic works like *Naughty Nights in Montmartre* will appreciate the title they gave the company which they formed – *Jamais Deux Sans Trois*.

Their novel invention would at once constitute a comfortably appointed meeting place for serious and only occasionally interrupted intercourse and cross-germination of ideas. Economy of lighting, heating and cleaning costs would flow. The saving in man hours alone would be significant. It need not be long before televisions, fridges and microwave ovens would be installed and small social gatherings could be arranged. In a word, as Kenith, flushed with success, said modestly, 'It's a small step for Tufnell Parc, a giant leap for Man United'. Unhappily, as we now know, the brilliant concept went the same way as the everlasting safety match. Luddites and nihilists with powerful vested interests branded the facility as otiose; it failed for want of influential support and was discarded. But not before its fame had spread to far-flung outposts of the Empire like Milton Keynes where, even as I write, its installation is still under debate. Whatever its fate, the brothers Rowsbury had brought a whole new meaning to the polite enquiry 'Are you sitting comfortably?'

Owen's brought distinction not only in industrial technology but in the arts as well. I was reminded of an example only last week wherein our intervention gave the world immortal works of classical music. At an auction in Sotheby's on Thursday last, a frame allegedly with a thin lock of Mozart's brown hair and a thick greying lock of Beethoven's, sold for £11,000. I recall vividly the family chronicle of the part played by my Great Great Uncle Max in the establishment of the genius of these two celebrated composers. It came about in this way. Uncle Max was educated at Owen's in the 1700s. They didn't actually say that he was untrustworthy but it is recorded that he achieved a name for himself there as he sought to prove that the shortest way between two points was a curve. He was himself something of an infant prodigy at the piano. He also had a violin and was described in his end of term report as no mean fiddler. In fact, his violin and his piano were by Stradivarius and Bechstein; unfortunately, the violin was by Bechstein and the piano by Stradivarius. His time at Owen's was abbreviated when he was invited to leave through an incident that was apparently connected with the headmaster's wife wherein young Max displayed outstanding virtuosity for a thirteen-year-old. The details are rather obscure but at the request of the Islington *gendarmerie*, he returned his attentions to the piano and soon became well known as a virtuoso on the instrument and had frequent occasion to visit the Continent and especially Vienna, and came to know both Wolfgang Amadeus Mozart and Ludwig von Beethoven well. Indeed, on first-name terms with them, he called them Wolfie and Lou respectively; they apparently called him Mucks.

They were all buddies and spent most of their time in Vienna and Paris, painting the towns red. Thanks to Uncle Max's influence, night was for womanizing, revelry and debauchery, together with a few other reprobates, earning the group the title of the Vienna Ratpack. Franzi Haydn was rather standoffish and kept himself to himself. May he rest in peace but it is a fact that some people actually say that Franzi's works were really tidied up by Uncle Max. Never mind, *De mortuis nil nisi bonum*, 'Arry, as Frank Bruno always says.

What with the high frenetic life pattern, it was hardly surprising that Lou found his hearing deteriorating. Max thought it was a wonder that his visual powers hadn't also grown weaker considering that Lou's activities as a boy at school had led to a warning that he might go blind. It was inevitable that the three were incessantly without funds when it was time to pay the rent. At this point Max, the only member of the pack with commercial sense, would dose Wolfie and Lou with dollops of black coffee and prop them up at the piano, to have Wolfie dash off a couple of concertos and a requiem (and if he had no afternoon bedroom assignments, an opera or two – hence *Don Giovanni* and *The Magic Flute*) and Lou to write a symphony which, despite distractions, Max insisted that he should make a point of finishing (a discipline his countryman Schubert later neglected). Max would then rush the compositions round to the local HMV office and sell them for a few gold louis. Thus, they barely staved off the creditors while some of the world's greatest musical compositions were born for future generations to adulate. All due to Owenian Uncle Max.

You may well ask what of the locks of hair at Sotheby's. Well, Max's diaries suggest that contrary to the auction particulars, Wolfie Mozart's hair may have had a reddish tinge, while young Lou's was distinctly sparse; in fact, he was not only pretty deaf but he had dandruff too (*vide Hairy Tales*, Horace Skillfuttock, 1923). That's something the musical historians don't mention. We are not told whence these tresses were plucked so we cannot further test the apparent inconsistency, but writing as one with his own thatch under threat, and with Wolfie and Lou both thinning on top, I ask you, reader, is it likely that they would have been passing round their locks so generously? No, bearing in mind Uncle Max's commercial bent and the buddies' propensity for practical jokes, would it not have been typical of these rascals, after a midnight supper of sauerkraut and brioches with several flagons of rough wine, to have hatched a scam to pay the barber at the Gare de Lyon Post Coach Station for a few locks of hair from his floor sweepings and then to have Uncle Max take them to one of his friends, a hair collector with a stall in London's Caledonian Market? This worthy would have labelled them as of Mozart and Beethoven origin and disappear after taking a decent profit (a case of hair today and gone tomorrow). Let me be clear, I am not impugning either Wolfie's or Lou's integrity; they were good ol' boys and anyway some of my best friends are musicians. But the scenario is not impossible, is it?

However that may be, you will observe, dear reader, that it is an Owenian, Uncle Max, to whom the world owes the priceless gift of some of its never-to-be-forgotten musical works – as well as an old antique frame.

As to Max's latter days, his lifelong exuberance turned melancholic and he became weary; his skill with the spinet became *vieux chapeau*. It seems that he blamed himself for having hastened Wolfie Mozart's tragic early passing in 1791 and he was greatly upset. His distress was the greater when Lou feigned total deafness when asked for a contribution towards the funeral expenses. So he came home. Contemporary reports have it that he was hanged as an incorrigible rogue around the year 1800. Another source alleges that the headmaster eventually caught up with him and gave him 100 lines. In an exceptionally painful place. I can divulge that in fact, he died at the age of 92 of natural causes, that is in his own bed with a pert little seamstress of nineteen. It was the traditional Owen's code of meeting any challenge. He had declined in his later years with the strain of constant crossings of the Channel with a packet. He had opened a jellied eel shop in West Ham but he lost interest when he found to his disappointment that piped harpsichord music by Mozart was unpopular with the customers. His funeral was attended by just under 20 young women who claimed current close companionship and countless small children, all of whom bore a remarkable resemblance to him. Owen's would have been proud.

There are very many examples of ways in which Owen's men and women have changed the course of history from the seventeenth century on. Historians speak and write glibly of the French Revolution and the Declaration of Human Rights but do they ever give due attribution to Owen's in these cataclysmic events? I fear not. Yet, it was in this highly charged atmosphere among the citizens of France in the year 1789 that it was an Owenian expedition that provided the spark to detonate the troubles. It happened in this way.

The French were impatiently awaiting the long-planned, first-ever cricket tour by an English side, arranged for the summer. The squad was actually en route but was turned back at Calais when news came of rioting in Paris. It can now be disclosed that the disturbances were at the instance of none other than a party of some of the most distinguished Owen's personnel of the day, who, accompanied by some other English supporters of similarly genteel upbringing, were come to cheer on their countrymen at the *Stade des Colombes*. The party was led by Lemuel Williamson and included such as the Rowsburys, Pietro de Salisbury, Raoul Coombes, Alongo Hunter, Tedeus Cuk, the Flucqs and former headmaster Gerard Jonas. All were in high spirits and eagerly looking forward to the weekend trip. They had arrived in Paris overnight and fuelled by sack, cheap French export lager and local plonk, bedecked in Union Jack scarves, bell-ringing and whistling, fists in the air, determined to give a good impression of the Briton abroad, marched down the *Champs Elysées*, chanting 'England for the Tasse' and "Ere we go, 'ere we go, 'ere we go' to the tune of the *Marseillaise*. Not unreasonably, they could not help knocking over a few lampposts, tables and chairs and affectionately kicked in the glass fronts of some cafés and boutiques on the way. Seizing the berets of some startled Parisians to play handball with was a lot of fun. Some of the less inhibited managed to throw a barouche into the pond in the *Jardin des Tuileries* and set fire to a hay cart while their companions rolled a barrel of manure into the midst of the startled diners in the cellar of the *Brasserie Alsacienne*. A heavily-bejewelled lady of the night lost her pitch and her cool as she sailed involuntarily through Fouquet's window.

At this stage of the proceedings, two of the school staff who taught biology, Johannes Sparrow and Eion Bries, who had come to extend their practical studies with a couple of nights of erotic lambada dancing, joined the march. Sparrow also intended to visit his cousin, Jean Moineau. To assist their work and ensure against being lonely, the two men were accompanied by two demure lovelies, Alice Schnorrer, a Swedish au pair, and Lola Bonk, a barmaid from Peckham, a pair themselves dedicated to the enlargement of human awareness. Meryl Streep and Katharine Turner they were not, but then, it was their minds that the men admired. They said.

What happened next is not entirely clear but it seems that a crowd of French citizens, disgracefully badly behaved and garlicked to the eyebrows, began to swarm up from *Les Invalides*, belching out clouds of Gauloise smoke. They were out to celebrate after a game with a curious-shaped ball that was destined later to be called rugby. One or two of them may have been inebriated. As they caught sight of the advancing Owen's-led contingent at the *Rond Point*, the word spread that the incursion was the vanguard of an English invasion. Still smarting from having to cede Canada in 1763, the natives hurtled into the attack with cries of *'Jamais les Anglais'* and *'Assassins'*, some waving muskets, pikes and cudgels while others brandished French loaves, pots of country paté, *petanque* balls and any other weapons available. One of those screaming the loudest was driving a horse-drawn 2CV, a small excitable pudgy-faced youth on a day-trip from Corsica, with a carnival admiral's hat on his head, comically knocked askew, who seemed to fancy himself as the leader. Name of Bonaparte. He was mouthing off something about the English being a nation of shopkeepers but screamed even louder as the athletic Bries performed a kind of triple salchow as he legged him into the fountain. One of the smaller Frenchmen sank his teeth into Dallas Rose's leg and quickly learned that the distinguished OO Dallas Rose was not a species of Texan flora as he suddenly found himself impaled on the business end of a café table umbrella. Yet another combatant was dragged away unconscious after he unwisely kept hammering Beau Shepherd's knee with his head.

Several thousands more appeared swiftly from nowhere to join the fight on both sides. Confusion reigned as the mêlée developed into a royal punch-up, then a fully fledged battle and finally to a war, with French fighting French amidst guttural shouts of *'Nom d'un chien'* ('Here, Rover') and *'Zut alors'* ('Well I never') from one side and 'Up Owen's' from the other. Insurance assessors arrived promptly, armed with tape measures and forms in triplicate to deal with claims. That night, casualties were heavy, the *Café des Puces* was stormed and the Bastille fell.

Lemuel Williamson had thrust his way to the front of the English battalion, calling 'come on, Frog, make my day. Fire that musket'. They bore in on him, belching such potent fumes of pure garlic, *soupe de poissons* and stale beer that his head swam and he was obliged to detach himself momentarily from the mass of struggling humanity and pause for breath. As he did so, he cried out 'You Frogs are really revolting'. It so happened that the noted news hawks, Jonsonian James Boswell and Owenian Ivan Waterhole, were stood nearby to hear Lemuel's cry and mistaking his meaning, they headed the copy they were sending to the *London Times* by the morning pigeon 'The French Revolution'. And that, gentle reader, is the way in which *'Les Evénéments de* 1789' officially became for posterity 'The French Revolution'. Once again, Owen's inspired.

With the clarity that is bred with the passage of time, we discern that the roots of the Declaration of Human Rights grew with the foundation of Dame Alice Owen's School and why not, for where else did the principles of liberty, equality and fraternity first proudly show their heads? Once again, Owen's had changed the course of history. *Les misérables* without bread were now getting double portions of cake instead, thanks to us (Marie Antoinette assisting).

Happily, the Rowsburys escaped the carnage of the people's takeover and later emerged from hiding to settle *chez* Mesdemoiselles Schnorrer and Bonk. After some rather physical negotiations with their French counterparts, the girls had secured places beside the guillotine to do a little knitting and what with the sale of some pullovers they produced and one or two other semi-public services that occurred to them as nice little earners, managed to scrape together enough to keep them all. Here again, let it be recorded that Owen's genius came to the surface. Let it be known that it was the legendary Rowsburys' skill that developed the prototype of the guillotine in 1792. It was not, repeat not, Joseph Guillotin who was responsible although he falsely claimed the credit. Guillotin was only an old acquaintance who had met the Rowsburys years before on one of his trips to London with his cycle and a few strings of onions draped round his shoulders. Guillotin even had the cheek to claim the royal warrant of the device which had given poor King Louis XVI the chop.

Kenith would have seen him off but was preoccupied at the time with his work on the development of the lavatory chain, an invention with which he had been experimenting for many years. The sad truth is that this would have been his *chef-d'oeuvre* but a tiny misplaced decimal point in his workings caused him to miss by a mere whisker a coveted place in the hall of fame. He it was who had set up the entire public structural presentation of combined cistern and specially warmed seat and, being a perfectionist, had himself assumed a natural position at the official opening at the *Palais des Sports* before the President and several thousand distinguished guests. A fanfare of raspberries heralded the rise of the curtain; Kenith gave a short address, assuring his audience that he was sitting comfortably, and gave the signal for a drum roll. The suspense was exquisite. Unfortunately he had erred in calculating the weight-bearing factor of the water in the cistern and as, to cheers and deafening applause, he pulled the chain, the entire kit and caboodle crashed down onto his head. He was caught, as they say, with his pants down. He perished of a fractured skull. He had not even patented his idea. I believe that, 30 years later, the eponymous Thomas Crapper claimed the credit, the fame and the fortune for it.

As for Paulinus, he became a chartered accountant and of course ended his days as a pauper.

So, I've drawn aside the veil over some of the numinous and too little-known intellectual, engineering and artistic contributions to mankind to have come from Owenian talent. Space in this journal does not permit of a fuller catalogue which may have to await propagation later. The parts played by distinguished O's like Jaime Everton, noted for his delicate china saucer designs and so the subject of the cry heard as far north as Merseyside of 'Everton for the Cup', Keith Freeman for his mysterious expeditions to the Central American hinterland and the import to this country of the Mexican Wave, David Greenshields for his pioneer work in bringing trading stamps to the British public, and esoteric literary classics like Barry Payne's work at Southgate on *Kebabs of the Ancient Greek Civilizations*, have brought lustre to the name of Owen's.

We may well be proud.

10

WHAT THE PAPER SAYS

To be dejected, furiously angry and modestly complacent at one and the same time is an unlikely mix.

As all my friends know, I'm a quiet, uncomplicated, even-tempered man, not easily shaken, but today, I've been shaken, and stirred as well, into an amalgam of the three above-mentioned sensations. And for three good reasons.

The day began in the usual way, that is to say I awoke (at my time of life, an achievement in itself). As is my wont, I turned first to the morning paper and scanned the death announcements to see if my name was there. It wasn't, so I got up. I celebrated my survival by falling on a light breakfast of juice, cereal, eggs, sausages and tomatoes, buttered toast and a large pot of coffee, and then turned back to the newspaper where three items caught my eye.

The first, which was the one that reduced me to a state of deep dejection, was the report of an address by an eminent literary scholar in which he deplored the contemporary decline in the quality of English grammar. He pointed particularly to the lack of respect for syntax and spelling, and the appallingly exiguous teaching of where and when to deploy apostrophes and commas. He went on to complain of the frequent misuse of the past participle in mistake for the past definite and instanced the case of 'shrunk' for 'shrank', 'sunk' for 'sank', and so on. He lamented the proliferation of split infinitives. To which

I could add the offensive mispronounced 'ekcetera' instead of 'etcetera' and the frequent improper employment of the 'I' in 'between you and I'. He had actually come across teacher graduates who were unsure if the word 'kudos' was singular or plural.

To those of us who have enjoyed our orthoepy at Owen's School and are still in love with the English language, this exposé can only be profoundly depressing. To realize that respect for the purity of language and the discipline of grammar is fading fast and is neither a source of pleasure nor an arm for the conveyance of precise meaning, is yet another sickly turn of the screw. Sad, sad, sad.

The second item was even more grave and my sorrow quickly gave way to anger. In fact, I nearly choked on my All Bran when I read it and turned so purple that my wife briefly suspended the day's telephone conference with her dressmaker, an event quite unprecedented. The piece tucked away at the foot of the page reported that the French union of ski instructors, out of work through lack of winter snow, are threatening the use of force to stem the influx of British 'amateur' instructors; unemployment among the French instructors is laid firmly at the door of the British. Now, I'm sorry about the skiing problems. I know that there are two supreme sensations in life – and skiing is one of them. But they go too far. What you might call trouble on the piste. A proud people, the account continued, on the principle of an eye for an eye they are threatening to send people across the Channel to infiltrate our national sport. Can they possibly mean, would they dare to target, English cricket? A national institution. This would be tantamount to a declaration of war, the collapse of the Anglo-French entente and an invasion of human rights. You can see why I'm irate.

Unexpected indeed are the recent changes of political ideologies in a Europe in the throes of realignment and separatism, the Oder-Neisse Line and the rest – however,

I confess that I have not viewed these signals as the end of civilization as we know it and I've been able to take them on board with the equanimity and resignation that come with great age. But an invasion of our game by Gallic barbarians would be no less than apocalyptic. We are getting used to swallowing all kinds of European diktats but when we smell interference with cricket, we do not turn the other cheek. French cricket played with young ladies when we were small was a lot of fun, but that was then, this is now.

Picture a typical scenario. The game starts as the French fielding side drift casually from various parts of the ground and naturally shake hands with each other. Soon, the umpire, Dickie Oiseau by name, clad in a fashionable shoulder-padded Cardin coat, impeccably coiffed, Gauloise drooping from lower lip, allows an appeal by the bowler by blowing a whistle. He pronounces sweetly to the batsman *'Va t'en, chéri, tu es dehors. You 'av ze canard d'or'*, whereupon the keeper runs up to the bowler and kisses him on both cheeks. The batsman, knowing that only a blind man could have failed to see that the ball would have missed the *jambe* stump by about a half metre, splutters a recommendation to the umpire to see a taxidermist and hollers *'Balles! Tu es fou. Et aussi aveugle. Up le tien, grenouille emmerdé.'* And if I were the batsman, I would have used the stump to deal the heathen a terminal blow across the throat.

And for tea, be sure that our statutory fish paste sandwiches, noisome but beloved, would go and in their place would be a plate of snails. Yes, I know it's said that snails have definite aphrodisiacal properties and that's okay at the right time and place, but how do we proceed with the game after tea if half the team is missing on the job and we first have to mount a search behind the pavilion and probably throw a few buckets of cold water over certain characters and dose them with bromide before we can take the field again. And then, much the worse for wear. Moreover, I have a strong feeling that after the game, two or three pints of Pernod do not quite fit the Botham image.

Cricket is as English as roast beef. The jargon of cricket is eclectically English. Bowling a maiden over is crystal clear but *'jetant une vierge á la terre'* is another matter. And if, which heaven forbid, cricket broadcasting is handed over to French TV, long on stylish graphics and futuristic images but short on play, you might as well give up.

And what would be the next institution to go? *The Archers* to be broadcast in Serbo-Croat? Is the National Anthem to be re-tagged 'God Save The Swiss'? You never know. Can you trust a people who can produce a character like Flaubert, celebrated for a propensity for sexual intercourse in public while fully dressed and smoking a cigar, who then try him for obscenity and acquit him? And subsequently actually award him the Legion d'Honneur (and, no doubt, a French kiss). That kind of licence doesn't leave much room for what used to be naïvely reckoned a steamy full frontal 'streak' across the Lord's wicket.

It may or may not be true that the French wear socks in bed and do not clean their teeth, but there is no denying that they have the traditional hot Gallic ill-temper, so we can expect punch-ups that will make the Gatting/Shakoor confrontation look like a playful spat. I once witnessed a turbulent scene in a village square in Provence. What had been a peaceful game of boules suddenly erupted into a war when one of the bouleurs formed the view that he was not being fairly treated. Even in repose, he did not make an attractive figure; for one thing, his arms were longer than his legs. But as the argument became more heated, his rage grew and he turned into a wild animal. Mayhem loomed. I certainly wouldn't have gone into a room with that ruffian if I'd had a whip and a chair, let alone face him on a cricket pitch. Man, I can tell you, I was out of there like a ship off a shovel.

For the roots of my introduction to the joyous arcana of cricket, I hark back to my early school days. As a third former, between the wars, I began my love affair with the game. On Field Day, we used to clamber noisily aboard the pirate bus and climb to the open top deck while it careered on a wild journey from the Angel to Oakleigh Park, weaving maniacally in and out of traffic to pass its more sedate General Omnibus rival. If it was raining or even snowing, the only protection on the upper deck was a tarpaulin cover which could be buttoned over our laps. I recall that to one shrewd third former, this was a boon because he would hide under the tarpaulin when the conductor eventually ascended heroically to collect fares. This earned him a saving of two old pence a week, a stratagem that probably began his route to fame and fortune for you will not be surprised to learn that he is now one of our distinguished Old Boys, very rich and a pillar of the community.

It has to be admitted that other boys, especially overgrown seniors, also capitalized on the occasions when the conductor failed to mount the spiral stairway to the open deck. Some of the attempts to find him and press the fare into his hand at the journey's end were less than fullhearted.

Although I was given my colours, football had no great hold on me. I relied on Sir Thomas Elyot who in 1531 concluded that it is 'to be utterly abjected of all noble men, nothing but beastly furie and extreme violence'. I agreed. My heart was given to cricket. I was fascinated by the contest that was so testing and thoughtful, yet so relaxed and uniquely satisfying in its atmosphere of quiet gentleness. I do not boast great talent but I am having coaching (Wigmore Club net and facilities) and next year, who knows? Last year, I had a batting average of 1.4; this year I have not been so successful. In fact, the only runs I got came from a vindaloo curry I had one Saturday night in Camden Town. Simon Raven has percipiently defined a true gentleman as a man who, when he has accepted an invitation to play, turns up at the ground even though it's raining. That sums it up for me. A possibility of the game falling into the hands of the old enemy is anathema. I would transmogrify from a gentle soul into a militant chauvinist in defence. If patriotism is rightly said to be the last resort of the scoundrel, you can call me Bugsy.

As for the third news item, to stir in my breast a comforting and a forgivable feeling of modest complacency, as befits a man who has made a remarkable discovery, it was the report of a recent American survey under the heading 'Sex Makes You Happy'. The subtext was to the effect that 'Grumpy people are less attractive and therefore less likely to have sex'. At first glance, some might call this twaddle. I prefer to recognize it as a revelation, possibly of greater importance to mankind than Einstein's Theory of Relativity. And much easier to follow. So, if you should spot a jokey chap strolling down the high street with a jaunty step, a maturish kind of Jack the Lad, huge facial smile fixed as if with superglue, whistling to one and all, bright as a butcher's dog, in a word a man just exuding good will, the most unmistakeably ungrumpy fellow in town – that's me.

It's clear that I've had it all wrong up to now. Like Sinatra, I did it my way; now, out with the black dog. I've been naïvely operating on a psychological technique that if you look forlorn and unhappy, you awaken her motherly instincts and she'll do anything to comfort you and come across. If you cry a little, in my theory, that's even better. And quicker. But it emerges that I was off-beam. This new slant explains what I have always thought was only bad luck. Ah, if only I'd known then.

11

THE BIRDS ARE SINGING AND I HEAR GYPSY VIOLINS WHEN YOU SMILE AT ME

Let me warn you, reader. This is a story of man's inhumanity to man, not fit for those of a nervous disposition, a tale that tells how even the basic ethic of sport and fair play is fickle. Remember the Hungarian count on a country weekend who remarked to his English host, 'How I love these sporting games. We so enjoy shooting peasants.' 'Not peasants, old man, they are pheasants,' replied his host gently. 'Look, old chap,' said the count, 'You have your customs, we have ours.' The moral is *'tout ça change, c'est la même chose'*. You must understand that the code of cynical tactics and quasi-cheating which we now see, including intimidation by bouncer and the batsman instead of the wicket as the target, is not new. It has been extant over the past 100 years since WG Grace was shamelessly deploying his own rules. And doubtless before that, in fact. Cricket is now a very serious business, too serious to be left to cricketers. We British must come to terms with the unpleasant reality that sport has become prey to venal influences. Winning is all. But this is no new phenomenon for the concept that it is not who wins or loses but how you play the game has long been old hat in some quarters.

My memory is scarred by the ordeal of a first real encounter with fear on the field of sport. Not that I am a coward. We all have personal idiosyncrasies; it just happens that one of mine is that when faced with a threatening situation, my face takes on a greyish hue, I sweat heavily and need to have frequent access to the pavilion facilities. My condition is well known to doctors as the Gevaltschrecker's Yellow Streak Syndrome.

I must be frank and admit that I had opted to play for Owen's on the day in question because I had once again been passed over by the Test selectors. Gubby Allen told me later that the sticking points were threefold – petty jealousy, internal politics and whether I would last the four days; even if I did, there was a general consensus of opinion that my World War II boots would not. (In parenthesis, let it be noted that they are still lasting well).

The Saturday afternoon of which I write was dark and sultry. Cars had their lights on, the atmosphere was heavy and the ball was swinging wildly with an uneven bounce on a bumpy pitch. The occasion was a 'needle' match with a neighbouring and regular arch enemy in our fixture list. I found my opposite number, a crapulent Mexican-moustached swollen-gutted pork butcher named Roland who, having unsteadily negotiated his way from a liquid lunch at The Fiddler's Elbow, was now located at the bar in the clubhouse. I pointed out courteously that we were already 30 minutes late. He fell off his stool and appeared to produce a coin; I called and he announced that I could take first knock. I was loath to upset him and assumed that I had lost the toss. I said to him carefully, 'With great respect,' (that preamble means 'You are a stupid clot but...'), 'I haven't had the privilege of seeing the coin.' He was already heading for the telephone and a transaction with his bookie.

The porcine skipper donned the wicket-keeper's pads and, with the motley crew constituting his eleven, took the field. It was then that I recognized with tragic suddenness their star bowler who was preparing to open the attack. He emerged from the pavilion carrying a pint in each hand. The style of his cricket wear was not just bizarre, it would have made Bob Geldof look elegant. To my horror, he was wearing a dingy 'Five Times A Night' T-shirt, doubtless a reference to cramp in the leg. I knew him of old, but he seemed somehow to have grown bigger and uglier. He replicated a savage reportedly recently found in the hinterland of Papua New Guinea, 8 feet and 3 inches tall. He was not everyone's favourite. Views expressed about him had been many and various, but a fair sample selection was that he was an un-Christian, mean, vicious, humourless ruffian with a prodigious animal strength and boasted an enormous wide open space between the ears. It was particularly disappointing to me as I felt that I had only just got the hang of elderly slow bowlers. I don't recall his name, but let us call him Rottweiler. How to describe him? First, he wore a permanent scowl; he was no Adonis. In fact, he was barrel-chested and built like a brick shipyard. His eyes were not standard brown or grey, they were sullen and red. A gold earring dangled from his left ear. A bullet-shaped cranium with close cropped hair *à la* French Legion (his barber must have used a gang mower) housed a potential head-butt of GBH proportions. His countenance was creased into hard uncompromising lines. If invited to guess his work, a *What's My Line* panel would have put him down as an axe murderer with perhaps a nice little sideline in kneecapping. He displayed all the charm and charity of a goon from the Khmer Rouge. With haemorrhoids.

To be fair, dear reader, you will agree that behind a rough exterior often lurks a person with warmth and a natural grace, a lovable directness, generosity and scholarship, with an endearing concern for the less fortunate among us. Rottweiler had none of these. Any resemblance to persons living or dead was purely coincidental. I felt we were looking at a man who had shaken hands with the devil. I can tell you, even if he'd ordered me out of a parking space I'd just occupied, I'd go fast. And raise my hat. It is not as if he were just hostile, he was homicidal. His philosophy was plainly, 'Let's do it to them before they do it to us.' I can't pinpoint it but I just had not taken to him. I had an instinctive feeling that he was not one of nature's gentlemen; I rationalized that perhaps I had caught him on a bad day, but my suspicions were confirmed when I saw that the tattoo across his forehead read, 'I Am A Bastard'.

Thus it was that Rottweiler opened from what can only be described as the darker end, that is the one with the thick clusters of foliage directly behind his arm. There were no sight-screens. He took no interest in the preliminaries of placing the field and from a 25-yard run, began a headlong rush like a bat out of hell. He should have faced a charge of aggravated assault. From his first delivery which, for all we could tell, could have been with a cannon-ball, he made it clear that he was taking no prisoners. His pact with the devil included a clause for the temporary suspension of the laws of inviscid dynamic velocity. He fired a projectile that struck Fred Roome a sickening thud amidships. Fred's eyes bulged and it shook a filling out of his tooth. He is now celibate.

My orders to our opening batsmen were to play a straight bat, not to worry about runs, just to contain the situation for the first ten overs or so. In the event, stumps were flying and splintering like matchwood from the word go. Within ten minutes, Rottweiler had removed the first four batsmen, some of the cream of our batting strength like Fred Roome, Dennis Elston, Len Mitchell and Norman Dommett. The medium-pacer from the other end (only Fred Trueman speed) was a merciful instrument sent to give them brief spells of respite. So eager were they to escape the fury from Rottweiler's end that both batsmen sought sanctuary and were once found sheltering together at the other end. The score was now four (byes) for four and it was my turn – the moment of truth.

Now, as I have indicated, I am not one for false heroics. My stomach refuses to play its part. From the corner of my eye, I could see the four batsmen who had been returned to the pavilion; they all seemed to be needing assistance with their breathing and they all seemed grateful to be alive. Roome was twitching in a corner, Elston was visibly shaken like a man who had seen an unnameably terrible vision, Mitchell's hair had turned white and Dommett was retching and barking behind the pavilion. So it was not easy to keep up my air of devil-may-care, Bond-type bravado as I prepared to stride out to the wicket. The truth, to which I have to admit strictly between ourselves, was that beneath the rippling biceps, the fine-tuned, superbly fit exterior and the mind of quicksilver, I was absolutely paralysed with fear. The trouble was that my legs were strangely refusing to propel my frame. My brow was clammy, my bowel loose. I toyed with the idea of pleading an attack of malaria or a sudden bereavement. Or of simply running away. I was conscious of having been guilty of a number of errors. First, in losing the toss (if I had), then in remaining sober and, above all, in being there at all. How foolish I'd been, I reflected, in leaving behind the African ju-ju I always carry for protection since I once had an unpleasant brush with a witch-doctor in Sierre Leone. Just because I called him a berk, he threatened to shrink my head, I have an idea that he'd made a start on my legs before I got away. With the ju-ju my host gave me and a potion made from a pint of goat's urine, I could have transformed Rottweiler into a gentle giant, even a princess if I'd got the right mixture. I only had to make it look like lager.

I cogitated whether I would be wise to wear a helmet but decided that even if I had an entire suit of armour, it would afford me little defence against Rottweiler in full flight. There was nothing I could use to fend him off, unless it was a black suspender belt, if the rumours I've heard about macho men are true. Anyway, I didn't have one. A helmet, I mean. What I needed was to be metamorphosed, like Aos of old, into 'all stones and hardness'. However, the fielding side was beginning openly to exhibit signs of impatience and their captain was talking of sending out a search party for the next man in, so I managed to unlock my legs and, with all the eagerness of a turkey summoned to a Christmas club draw, I strode out to the wicket. My passage to the square was a deeply religious journey – I prayed all the way. I also sang, *When The Saints Go Marching In* to myself to keep my spirits up. I remember that soon after, when I came back, I was singing, *No One Knows The Trouble I've Seen*.

It was then that I made my last and biggest mistake. On the spur of the moment, I decided that it would be a good idea to ingratiate myself with Rottweiler and perhaps to trigger some unexpected fund of charity. As I came abreast of him I said cheerfully (although it came out of my mouth in a strangely choked voice) 'Good afternoon, squire'. It was quickly clear that he was not used to civil exchanges with the enemy. My greeting did, in fact, have an effect; you get the same effect from a bull if you wave a red rag at him. His reaction was slow but positive. With undisguised contempt, he studied me from his great height much as a piranha would look at a sardine. With deliberateness, he ran his forefinger around inside his upper lip to locate and extirpate some debris from his mouth; then, with a mighty hawk, he activated a massive expectoration involving the withdrawal of a quantity of mucous from his pulmonary area and spat heavily onto my right newly-blancoed boot. It was what you might call one of the Great Expectorations. I think he was trying to make a point. He was obviously not prone to long speeches because it was in only four words that he gave me some advice that was unacceptable because it was both impossible of execution and lacking in relevance. This is a respectable work so that I shall not quote him verbatim. But I do realize now that with his reply he taught me a deeper understanding of human relationships. Anyway, he continued to stare hard, his eyes saying, 'You can run but you can't hide'.

I hyperventilated for a few moments. Then I resumed my progress to Death Row while he turned and stomped back to his mark at the pavilion steps. I passed Ron Nash who was miraculously still unscathed at the wicket and was awaiting my arrival. As I passed him, he murmured, 'Good Luck' and I thought sadly that I've had better luck with a chain-letter. My heart was beating so fast that an electrocardiogram at that point would have called for immediate embalming treatment.

The dance of death began. There were four balls to go. I tried to look nonchalant as I took guard and surveyed the field, pretending that I could see through the blurred image of my tear-filled eyes. I looked at him. He looked at me. He reminded me of nothing so much as an oversized grizzly who had scented a chance of supper. I believe he was actually panting. My mouth was completely dry. He thundered up to the lift-off site and, as he fired the missile, he emitted a sound that was something between a deep grunt and an agonized cry. I thought he also actually screamed like a Bulgarian shot-putter but they told me afterwards that the sound came from me, not him. At the same time, he broke wind. It was reminiscent of the Krakatoa volcanic eruption and I reckon it must have measured about 7.3 on the Richter scale.

I survived only three deliveries before he broke my hand. The first was overpitched and struck me on the toecap, proceeding on to the boundary unchecked such was the force of its propulsion. The excruciating pain in my foot was only matched in intensity by Rottweiler's anger when the umpire refused his appeal for leg before wicket. Our umpire was one Goff Phillips, a baseball devotee, a genial rotund figure, popular at Oakleigh Park. Goff was normally our own Number 11 bat, a character noted for phlegm and stolidity, more likely to be swayed by grit than logic. When he occasionally stood as umpire, he was always carefully rigged in a full-striped baseball outfit with red peaked cap worn back to front. He was equipped with the permanent affability of a yak and he was too thick to be scared of Rottweiler or any other monster. He was also famous for having once given a batsman out leg before wicket while standing at square leg. Goff was above all consistent; he made it a rule only to give a batsman out after every third appeal. Thus, as Rottweiler was only the first he did not qualify as eligible for a decision by Goff.

Rottweiler's megaphonic appeal for LBW was heard throughout North London. In fact, it shattered several glasses in the pavilion bar and woke an elderly spectator, Bert Poad, who had come to cheer us on. When Goff shook his head, Rottweiler looked in danger of a brain haemorrhage. He fell to his knees, clutching his head with both hands, then beating the ground with his fists in an agony of despair and indignation. Meanwhile, I was howling blue murder and hopping around, trying to bring back some feeling in my foot. The bowler rose at last and it looked as if Goff was in for a bloody nose, but he only addressed him briefly. I heard what he said and claim that it was out of order. After all, a man's copulative activity is not necessarily connected with his parents' forgetfulness of formal matrimonial arrangements, is it? However, it was very interesting because, for the first time since I'd known him, Goff blinked.

After an interval for my paralysis to descend again into unbearable pain, Rottweiler shot his second delivery at me. He missed me but scored a bull's-eye on the overweight wicket-keeper's throat, he being full of ale and not nearly nimble enough to skip out of the way. That worthy was laid low with his breathing only intermittent. I managed to restrain myself from an excessive display of grief at this case of the unspeakable in pursuit of the disagreeable. He'll have to take his beverages intravenously for a while, Ron told me uncharitably. Life-saving and mouth-to-mouth procedures were put in train, in which the bowler took neither part nor interest. I stayed on the fringe; I wasn't going to get caught up in the mouth-to-mouth proceedings. There was a further interval while Fatty was carried off and another brave fellow donned the keeper's pads to take his place, this time some 15 yards behind the wicket. The feeling was beginning to return to my foot, although obviously badly bruised, and I was composing myself when Rottweiler despatched his third delivery. He started his run and my blood froze as I saw he was smiling, it was the mirthless smile of an executioner. The ball made straight for my head like a rocket. I had time only for slight avoiding action and the ball clipped my left ear. I stayed upright but heard the birds singing and gypsy violins playing for a minute or so.

Now he was frustrated. He had tasted blood. I could see that he was planning something very special for me on the basis that he'd been put on earth to maim me or better, to separate my head from the rest of my body. We did not have to wait any longer for the end of this Kafkaesque nightmare. I am in no doubt at all that he summoned every malevolent ounce of strength at his command as he ran in. I swear I did not see the ball leave his hand. It reared off a short length and as I played back with bat high to shield my face, the ball, which was probably travelling at something near the speed of sound, struck my hand and fractured a metacarpal.

It was with a curious feeling of relief that I was escorted back to the pavilion. I felt that I'd outsmarted him in getting away without terminal injury or disfigurement. I was so elated at this achievement and with the comforting knowledge that I was actually on the way to the haven of the out-patients' department of the local hospital that I gave him a triumphant V sign as I passed him. I don't know what he made of it because I scuttled away to the safety of the pavilion.

The rest was anticlimax. The opposition were denied the victory they were scenting. God in his infinite wisdom decided that enough was enough. The heavens opened and, as I left the ground, a mighty storm broke. The field quickly became a quagmire and the game was abandoned. Even if they found oil, we would never visit the ground again. As to Rottweiler, it emerged later that he had played regularly for his county, but had opted to play in our game because he had to leave early. Doubtless to keep an engagement on an armed robbery. This denied us the pleasure of lacing his drink with cyanide after the abandonment.

I have recounted to you what was an exceptionally traumatic experience. It had been a day of cruel and unmitigated horror, anguish and infamy. The film of this dramatic story, shortly to be made, will star either Kenneth Branagh or Warren Beatty as myself, Sylvester Stallone as Rottweiler and (for demure love interest) Madonna as a tea lady/scorer. It will bring home graphically to the British public the crimes that are perpetrated, the barbaric codes that are insinuated, in the name of cricket. History will make the judgement. Yet, I must admit that my hair stood on end when I read in the local press that, 'The annual duel between these two old adversaries was renewed on Saturday at Popes Lane. It promised to be a keenly fought contest, played in a sporting spirit of friendly rivalry, but was unfortunately rained off.' Sporting! Friendly! What about a word or two on indomitable courage and devotion to duty on the part of certain persons while under intense enemy fire? The writer must be the same sportsman who's advocating dwarf tossing for the next Olympics.

12

THE TRUTH ABOUT PROFESSOR EINSTEIN AND HIS MATES (UNEXPURGATED)

While not going so far as to accuse me of being senile, there are some Old Owenians who suggest that, like King George III who shook hands with an oak tree under the impression that it was Frederick the Great, my lights are on, but there's no one at home. True, I am very old now, over forty, and can remember a time long ago when computer software meant an accountant's underpants and queer meant unwell.

Therefore, in the grand manner now common to aged and self-indulgent writers, I would like to tell of the advice my grandfather gave me when I was a lad at Owen's, I would like to say over a dinner of buttered asparagus, lobster and champagne soufflé, washed down with a light but respectable Chardonnay, at *Frascati*'s, but I would be lying. The fact is, however, that it was over a plate of sausages, beans and mash at a café in the shadow of Euston Station (massage and friendly dining). The wisdom of his counsel was none the worse for that. What he said can be distilled into few words. 'Son,' he said ponderously picking his teeth with a fork and carefully sorting some debris out of his beard. 'If you can't see it and you can't feel it, don't trust it.'

That he was subsequently relieved of his life's savings by two Germans who convinced him that a new scientific method of replicating crystal glass at one-tenth of the current cost was the way to a fortune, is beside the point. He forgot that he couldn't see or touch it. He wasn't bitter; he just brought down an old Lithuanian curse on them to cause them a double brain haemorrhage.

But the memory moved me the other day to thinking about the genuineness of scientific ingenuity. I may be eccentric but I confess I am a sceptic. Doesn't the record show that science runs into more problems than it solves? After all, when you get down to rock bottom, nearly all sciences are inexact. Wittgenstein, a fair judge, thought science unimportant. Moreover, he was appalled at some of the recent examples of its application. I remember long philosophical discussions with him and Russell when I eventually announced that I agreed with them. They were both much relieved, of course.

To develop my case, consider the outstanding scientific figure of this century, Professor Albert Einstein. He is said to have been 'a genius'. But do you know how fragile was that genius? Between these four walls, let me tell you he was defeated by the simple problem of socks. He would never under any circumstances whatever wear socks, no matter how important the occasion. 'Himmel, I found out that the big toe always ends up making a *verdammte* hole in the sock,' he complained, 'so I stopped wearing socks'. Thus spoke the man who perfected his light-quantum hypothesis with the equation $E = MC^2$ in between sessions at the Lucania snooker hall over Montague Burton's and trips to the betting shop. Sock shop owners could starve for all he cared. His feet were not only sockless, they were made of clay. Like many other powerful men, he also dallied with the ladies, but a predilection for sucking garlic tablets told against him. His old chum, Al Schweitzer, is reported as saying of Albie that he was 'a bit of a raver' and he didn't want to be a scientist; his ambition was to be a punk rocker like his grandfather. Not many people know that. He played a mean game of gin rummy with the boys in the lab but, frankly, one of his students, William Hamilton-Hinds, who rose to fame at Owen's says he talked an awful lot of scientific claptrap and even his most sycophantic colleagues began to tire of his old party trick with the litmus paper turning red. By the way, there was no truth in the rumour that William Hamilton-Hinds was the secret love-child of Einstein and Agatha Christie. Not many people know that either.

I recall clearly the age of pre-technology when I was at Owen's School before the promotion of advanced science and new technology by public relations hypesters. I was never good at chemistry or physics so that I confess humbly that I am not equipped to test the credibility of deeply arcane laws and theories proffered by reputedly brilliant minds. To me the school lab was a place of fun where we could make stink bombs and itching powder, test the effect of dropping chalk into ink-wells and observe the effect of the sun's rays focused through a magnifying glass on the dozing Soapy Grant's nose. I was to physics what Oliver Reed is to alcohol-free wine. I fear I caused Armitage to age prematurely and spent much time in detention instead of in serious experimentation. The school has proudly produced many distinguished scientists; I was not one of them.

A fortiori, a number of encounters with crackpots and cranks over the years have made me distrustful of science and scientists. Let me give you some examples. In the early 1970s, when the price of Middle-East oil rocketed, a chap named Grunt, an industrial chemist, purported to have found a substitute for petrol at a fraction of its cost, with a mixture, hitherto unconsidered, of camphor balls and vinegar. He invited me to place a mere £5,000 in a Swiss bank in exchange for the formula. At a demonstration, I noted that the mixture did indeed power the car's engine to travel half a mile. The catch was that it then blew up. Grunt admitted that this was a small problem he had forgotten to mention.

There was another, Dr O'Feeney by name, who boasted a doctorate in geology. He showed me a small lump of mushroom-coloured rock which had been uncovered in the course of an archaeological dig in an Irish bog. He averred that it was six million years and two days old. I was intrigued and asked him how he was able to date the rock so exactly. 'Simple,' he explained, 'the man who sold it to me gave me his word that it was six million years old, and that was two days ago.'

Now I learn that a cryobiologist in Eastbourne advertises an offer to freeze your dead body at −19°C until a cure is found for the condition that killed you. His charges are according to size with the price of £100,000 for the whole body or £50,000 for the head alone. Payment up front and no credit cards.

I'd be a willing convert if only they'd invent something really useful, some elixir to relieve some of the commonplace scourges of everyday life. For example, have you tried to reset a digital watch lately? Can you decipher station announcements on the tube platform? What about brain transplants for disc jockeys? Why not an antidote to the laws of gravity so that our noses don't drip when we have a cold? Think, ladies, but for gravity you could age without your face dropping into folds or wrinkles; chaps, you could get plastered without falling over. Let them apply their genius to solving the impact of relativity so that one day we'll be able to go back in time and put right the errors of the past. These are the sort of scientific discoveries that I would rate a real contribution to the human condition, far more valuable than the origin of the solar system or the *cui bono* revelation that it is the male sea-horse that becomes pregnant.

But no, they make everything so complex and esoteric. Take golf, a simple game. I read a treatise last week, written scientifically and in all seriousness, about the best way to hit a golf ball which is for the club to build up a dynamic pulling weight of 100 lbs during a 1.5 second motion, swinging at a speed of 90 miles per hour through an arc of approximately 18 feet. The ball, it stipulated, must be on the club face for just 0.00035 of a second and has to be launched at an angle of 42 degrees. Cobblers. I suspect that this pompous nonsense is going to put more potential golfers off than recruit them to the links.

I remember my own introduction to the game, many years ago, when I was aboard a ship that had put into Aden. It was at the hands of honest players who had never heard of the pretentious scientific approach. Incidentally, I was sporting a beard at the time and, on walking through the bazaar, I remember being greeted with cries of, 'Hey Isaac, you want good buy, immense profit'. My wife was greeted by 'Hey, Mrs Simpson, cheap bargain here for lady'. It was a memorable voyage in many ways, as I recall. A chap named Cohen fell overboard into the Red Sea but fortunately was saved. It was rumoured that he'd walked on the water to safety. However, to return to the point I was making about otiose scientific aids, our host took us to see the desert course where we found the bizarre spectacle of two Englishmen in plus-fours, bright green knitted sweaters, two-tone brown shoes and bobbled caps, briars clutched between teeth, unflurriedly playing eighteen holes. 'D****d glad to meet you, old chap,' said one. They drove off from the first tee into the Greater Yemen and followed up by camel. I believe the first hole (the short one) must have been about 180 miles long and had a bogey of 8000. Whilst we watched, I swear that one of them, before driving off, looked out into Saudi Arabia and actually shouted, 'Fore'. These uncomplicated expats played the game as it was intended. I believe they do still. They had no need of help from integral calculus.

Proof of the soundness of my doubts, if proof were needed, is that my wife, who is in the midst of a busy life what with, on the one hand, solving the Middle-East problem and on the other, the extermination of most of the wasp population of Great Britain, has now embarked on a course of study in the science of economics. I am sorry, but not surprised, to say that this has led to a claim that she is being underpaid by me. Coincidentally, I have for some time been considering having her arrested for demanding money with menaces or, better still, with attempted murder, because the latter is more likely and anyway carries a longer term of imprisonment. Watch this space.

13

A KICK IN THE VANITIES

I've been lucky. Without being unduly uxorious, I declare that I married a beautiful and desirable lady. That she chose me as her mate for life was the topic of much discussion in her family circle. I well remember her father abandoning the devil's brew for long enough to be assisted to his feet and make his speech at the wedding reception. 'We all wish the best for our children,' he declared, turning to look at me, 'and we never doubted that Marty would marry a chap who was tall, athletic, hardworking, handsome and rich....' He paused. 'But lo and be'old yer,' (his favourite attention-catcher) 'would you Adam and Eve it, she goes and finds a prat like 'im.' Bob, as you will deduce from his brand of deathless prose, was honest, direct and a formidable character but, contrary to the impression given to his fellow polemicists like 'Kneecapper' Ansell and Chummy Mancini (Chummy is the one who boasts membership of Alcoholics Unanimous, that's the society that guarantees if you don't feel like having a drink and you 'phone them up, they'll send someone round to persuade you to have one) in their Friday night debates in the *Black Boy*, my father-in-law was not at that time a professor of behavioural science, merely the Sage of West Green Road. Nonetheless, it is fair to say that neophytes came from all corners of Haringey and Wood Green to enjoy his delphic utterances and many guests at the reception, with the notable inclusion of the above-mentioned worthies, agreed that he had made a valid point. As I wrote in another place, Bob's family crest, prominently displayed on the fascia of his fish-catering emporia, featured three haddocks rampant over a pickled cucumber with the motto, 'Civility and Cleanliness'; I would admit under strong cross-examination that the 'Civility' had at times been known to be under strain but, nevertheless, comment from such a learned source was not to be ignored. I was shaken.

Now, many years on, I reflect on whether I had been making the most of the modest quantum of blessings Mother Nature had bestowed on me. The fear of a naturally ageing appearance has led many better men than I to the psychotherapist's couch. For one thing, there is hair; my hair coverage seems to have become disorientated and a plenitude of growth elsewhere may have drawn off some of the quota designed for the head. A generous head of hair with silver wings at the temples was ever an attractive feature in the male. An ungenerous ration, on the contrary, dulls a man's image. This is a generalization from which heroic superguys like Alan Hunter and Duncan Goodhew are, of course, excluded. But not only is there the cosmetic aspect, ordinary mortals only have to be hatless in the sun for an hour or two and the next thing you know, your crown fries and is scarred for life.

The crucial question is whether, while I'm waiting for the scientific breakthrough in the *in vitro* growth of human hair from male sex hormones and after nauseous experiments with such as bacon fat rubbings, I should purchase what is known among the Coopers Lane *hoi polloi* as a rug, an Irish or a barnet. In other words, a hairpiece or a toupee. I have noticed of late a thinning of my hairline that may give the impression of great age. Of course, this is a condition that has afflicted many famous figures all the way from Aeschylus down to Bobby Charlton and Norman Tebbit. In the latter's case, the line has fallen off the edge.

Socrates claimed that baldness was the result of too

much sex. Don't believe it. By and large, we men do not welcome the disappearance of our hair, although some claim indifference and simper about grass not growing on a busy street. However, broadcaster Robert Robinson was frank in interview; asked if he was shy about being bald, Robinson replied, 'Not shy; though if I could get hair to grow on my head by dipping my face in goose s**t, I'd do it.'

On a recent 747 flight over 12 tedious hours from Los Angeles, I engaged in an agreeable discussion with an acknowledged world authority on hair care and indeed on all aspects of cosmetic sophistication, Vidal Sassoon (I know, as the Queen Mother told me the other day, I really shouldn't name-drop). But I failed to draw from him any valuable tips to arrest my ageing process. This was doubly disappointing because, although we are of like age, he looks a superbly fit twenty-five years old while most of our fellow travellers reckoned I was his grandfather. But all I learned from him was that beauty comes from within and that that requires all aspirants to think beautiful thoughts. Of course, a face-lift helps too.

I once tried an experiment many moons ago when still not spoken for. The premature shedding of a few strands of hair set alarm bells ringing in my ego. I didn't aim to be a putative Mr Universe but I needed to banish self-doubt and convince myself that a thinning thatch need not signal the death of attractiveness and virility in the male. Up to this point, my experiences had not been such as to generate great self-esteem, but it was as a callow lad at Owen's School that it dawned on me briefly that an intelligently systemic approach to personal presentation might be important. I noticed that it was the better turned out of my peers who were finding favour with the staff and with their fellows. Save for those few whose brilliance overwhelmed their loucheness, the centre of power and the prizes in the classroom and on the field seemed to rest with the pupils whose persona was impressive and caught the eye. Researchers are now agreed that, whether just or not, some of us are more equal than others. The consensus is that the more attractive the presentation – an open, attentive, genteel mien, clear skin, even white teeth, and above all an appealing air of quiet but efficient magnetism – the more favourable the impact. For my experiment, I was prepared to assume the most complaisant of appearances. Now that I am so old that if I were a horse they would have to shoot me, I see it more clearly; when I was younger, I was slower to perceive this truism. The race is not always to the swift nor the battle to the strong.

Younger people should be taught to maximize their natural assets; there is nothing shameful in that. I recall a number of contemporaries at school in proof of the theory. They included Peter L. He was a contumacious youth with a good brain but an incorrigible oaf, prone to belch his contributions noisily in the classroom throughout sessions, without natural grace of any kind, louche in the extreme. Such was the ferocity and frequency of his disgusting interpolations from the back of the room that he may well have suffered from Tourette's syndrome; never introduced to the benefits of a brush or comb to regiment his head, his current style was of a shaven pate with just a two-inch long tuft of hair at the forehead. He wasn't lacking in courage, though; he died bravely on active service in World War II. Clifford S was another, a brilliant mathematician but unattractive and with mucky nose permanently in a state of gross ragamuffinery, filthy and unkempt. His tie would be knotted tightly and wound round to the side of his neck, his knees perpetually muddied and scratched, his socks holed and his shoes scuffed of leather; he wore a long striped scarf, whether hot or cold, indoors and out.

Then there was the mouse-like Percy C who carried with him a permanent stench of untended nether parts and fouled underwear (we used to spy on him over the top of the changing rooms at the Northampton Poly baths).

No, it was the DG Richardses, Gordon Dixons, Arnold

Haggers, Ronald Waldmans and the other clean-cut young men out of *Boys' Own*, who carried off the prizes.

My fumbling experiences after leaving school were unsatisfactory. For example, hungry for romance and a steady relationship, I was naïve about the initiative. I remember at college screwing up the courage one valentine's day to accost a fellow student I'd been secretly admiring all the year. She was truly desirable and I kissed her on the cheek (I didn't kiss her on the lips because I'd been told she might get pregnant that way) and gave her a valentine's heart as I breathed hoarsely at her, 'You know, I really, really like you.' She averted her eyes and replied crisply, 'Well, I don't like you, sucker, get lost.' Next day, adding insult to injury, her father complained to the Head about the need for disciplining students who were budding perverts.

Thus, having expended a large part of my slender income on jejune aids like Dr Sprinzelman's Pomade and Groper's Facial Elixir, culled from the weekend tabloid columns, I embarked innocently on my experiment. I togged myself out one Sunday morning in a carefully planned rig of what the well-dressed sporting *bon vivant* about town would wear to attract interest. I parked the car outside the Cricklewood Palais de Danse where the celebrated Sunday morning peacock parade was regularly played out. The scenario really called for a shiny red Ferrari Testarrossa but unfortunately I had to make do with a Reliant Robin ('Honest, guv, guaranteed genuine 60,000 miles only').

I think that my sartorial line merits a detailed description. I chose a sharp, double-breasted blazer in navy; I rejected one in duck-egg blue as being slightly over-the-top. My old school football colours showed up well on the breast (no one could work out what the intertwined black and red initials OSFC stood for but assumed them to represent an international badge for monocycling or some similarly arcane sport). The gold buttons contrasted perfectly with dignified denim trousers. I had, in fact, not intended to wear the drainpipe blue denims but an accident in the preparations the day before had put paid to my other trousers which were of white flannel. Anxious to look immaculate, I'd had the brainwave of securing a knife-edge crease in the flannels by enlisting the aid of Pip Berman, a client who was a veneered plywood manufacturer. Pip had a press in his factory that was used to power-fix the veneers to the boards to such an intensity that no human agency would ever be able to separate them. Pip guaranteed that if the flannels were placed in the press, a knife-edge crease would result. He omitted to mention that the press exerted pressure of some 3000 lbs per square inch. When he released the control lever, the flannels not only had a knife-edge crease but were now sliced crisply into two halves where the creases used to be. Like a knife through butter. Thus it came about that blue denims had to replace the white flannels in my ensemble. The denims were long past their sell-by date and had been bought some years before when I was sixteen as a special treat to be worn at my last Visitation and were now so extraordinarily tight in the crotch that they caused my eyes to bulge. In fact, they were so tight that they sprang a split in the pressure area when I raised my foot to the running-board of the Reliant, which gave some welcome relief and permitted normal breathing to be resumed.

An All England Lawn Tennis club foulard, purchased in Old Broad Street at an outfitters where there was no pretence of asking for credentials before selling eclectic club items, melded nicely with a fine twill shirt (M&S) open at the chest, black suede shoes and clocked socks. A straw boater and a red rose in my buttonhole that set me back sixpence at the flower seller completed an effulgent ensemble that may not have been Kilgour and French, but then it wasn't Oxfam either. I think that the word was natty, perhaps raffish. A light application of bronzer oil gave that fine-tanned skin look. I could not help noticing the curious glances of passers-by. After all, it was mid-

January and snowing. I congratulated myself on being what in B Cartland novels is called the cynosure of all eyes. I was satisfied that I had achieved the keynote of quiet good taste in my presentation and, as a tribute, I sprayed my head with a generous squirt of Cuban Rum eau-de-Cologne purchased from Maurice ('Something for the weekend, sir?), my barber in the little salon at the rear of the tobacconists in Holloway Road. I refused his offer of an earring as it would have been unwise to draw attention to the head. In any case, my ear hadn't been pierced. Oh yes, and I removed the Walthamstow dog track badge and left a Royal Ascot car park sticker (retrieved from the senior partner's bin the previous summer) on the window of the Reliant to show membership of the exclusive set.

I was now ready to prove that there is life after adolescence and that an English sporting hotshot prototype, even when showing some scalp, can make his mark. I believe that I exuded sang-froid as I posed with foot on running-board, puffing importantly on a curly meerschaum with hinged chimney. Here was a man with *savoir faire*, a man of the world. In the event, however, no significant progress was made. In fact, there were but two direct responses; one came from a cheeky youth on a bike who took one look and then wheeled around for a second. 'Saucy old sod,' he called. 'Looks like a pox doctor's clerk,' and rode off, thankfully nearly under the wheels of a bus. The 'old' hurt. The boy had no breeding.

The other was promising; an enchanting red-cheeked young lady, of about twenty, proudly bringing into view the sort of body that could have started a revolution, encased in black leather, a veritable goddess, raised my hopes as she changed course and came towards me, I had no doubt to ask me to father her children. She could have walked out of the pages of the top models register, except that she wasn't anorexic. She had big assets. The adrenalin flowed as I prepared myself for the initial gambit of suggesting a visit to Lyons tea shop for a pot of tea for two with toasted crumpets. But fate took an ugly turn.

She said something to her companion and I heard the words, 'Poor old chap,' as she smiled sweetly. Then she delved into her handbag and slipped a 10p coin into my palm. 'Here, buy yourself a cup of tea, dad,' she whispered and, before I could gather myself for a suitable reply, she'd squelched away into the slush. I pocketed the 10p.

I stayed at my post a little longer but was soon forced to take refuge in the three-wheeler for fear of an onset of hypothermia. Shortly after, a gang of thugs exited from the next-door pub and began to enjoy some intellectual exercise by violently rocking my Reliant; when they started to turn it over onto its roof, I left the scene. I have to tell you, sadly, that I could only draw one conclusion from the exercise, namely that sophisticated bearing, elegance and a pleasing appearance are not enough these days. Especially to counter a sparse mane. Even in a snowstorm. It must have been those damned denims. I might as well have stuck to the usual army surplus gear. The trouble is that the arbiters of taste in Cricklewood wouldn't know a pleasing appearance if they fell over one. I had failed, but gloriously. I toyed with the idea of drinking a bottle of lysol to end it all but, when I got home, I settled for a mug of cocoa.

14

LA PLUME DE MA TANTE

This is a chronicle of the first 24 hours of a short holiday in France from which I recently returned unscathed. I put it that way because it's a notable triumph to survive the carnage on the roads (and, for that matter, the pavements), especially if you're British (the French motorist has a nose for a British victim). That is, if you're not mugged first. While I was there, *Nice Matin* reported that an American woman whose tyre had gone flat on the RN7 was delighted when a French driver pulled up and offered to help. He jacked up the car, removed the tyre, took her purse and drove off.

When he heard I was going to vacation in France, a friend whose judgement I have learned to respect asked, 'Why on earth would anyone want to go to France? The French are a lot of breeders.' I didn't quite see the relevance of French procreational pastimes but I'm pretty sure that's what he said.

The fact is that there is an art to a successful stay in a French hotel. Bitter experience has taught me that there are four important canons to observe. The first is securing admittance at all, the second is minimum plumbing arrangements, the third is the competence of the television and the fourth is the adequacy of the soundproofing in the room. I have for some years patronized *L'Etoile Jaune*, a small hotel near Cannes in the South of France, ideally situated near to beach, hills and shops. I am well known there but as I addressed myself to the reception counter a few weeks ago, wearied by an uncomfortable and overlong journey, with French conversational dictionary and diarrhoea pills at hand, I had a presentiment of problems ahead. I was right. I was greeted, in the loosest sense of the word, by a tiny, thin-lipped, bird-like woman of a certain age, who emerged reluctantly from the Stygian gloom of a back office. Clad in black from head to toe, a Gauloise drooping from the corner of her mouth, she was the archetypal tragically ageing Edith Piaf with the refrain of *Non, Je Ne Regrette Rien* etched on her face. She was bedraggled, defensive and watchful, looking as if she'd just had sex with a bear. I noticed an empty bottle of pastis on the table behind her. She eyed me as warmly as she would a pit bull terrier with rabies. I'd never seen her before but this wasn't surprising because the *L'Etoile Jaune* management was not noted for the warmth of its staff relations nor the generosity of its pay scales. In fact, a fellow guest later alleged that the top pay was 500 francs a month and all you can steal.

After a perfunctory flip through a well-thumbed *circa* 1920 book, she told me coldly in French that there was no record of a reservation in my name. I was tempted to suggest that she was looking in the wrong set of books, the official one, and ought to take a look in the second set of books, the anti-VAT one kept in the secret drawer, but I decided that might be counter-productive. In any case, before I could protest, I was shouldered aside unceremoniously by three French women who swept up to the counter. My turn came again some 15 minutes later when the lobby had emptied of any other human presence and Edith Piaf acknowledged me with open hostility as I stepped forward. I tried a lame attempt at humour with the quip that all hotels keep a room vacant in case President Mitterand or some other VIP should turn up unexpectedly and I could assure her that he wasn't coming so could I please have that room. It fell on stony ground. She looked at me with a mixture of loathing and disgust – you'd have thought I'd asked her to tuck me up in her own bed and give me a cuddle.

She disappeared into the rear office again and reappeared in the wake of a large female with a blouse straining over a prodigious bosom and quality legs (oak-like with ball and claw feet), who looked as if she could eat E Piaf for breakfast, and probably had. This one was anything but a *fille de joie*, more like a Bessarabian weightlifter. There is a species of frog known as a Batrachian or laughing frog; she was definitely not of that genre. She was a founder member of the Down With Perfidious Albion club, if ever I saw one. She was patently not about to grace my arrival with a red carpet ceremony. In fact she looked me up and down as if I'd confessed that I'd strangled the Pope and snarled something. It must have been the French for 'We've got a right one 'ere'. She advanced in my direction, pretty clearly intending to dole out a spot of discipline. It dawned on me that ordinary pleas to reason or charity would be useless so I dug down into the conversational French I'd imbibed painfully from dear Henri Smith at Owen's two generations before and nervous, but ever plucky, I declared, distinctly and deliberately, *'Je suis anglais'*. La Piaf busied herself with some papers and continued to regret nothing but La Bosom blinked and checked at the forthright Anglo-Saxon declaration. Dredging up from the depths of my memory my last remaining Henri Smith French I went on, sternly, *'La plume de ma tante est sur la table.'* La Bosom, struggling to rationalize words that were obviously coded with a hidden meaning, stopped in her tracks and twitched like a wounded elephant. *'Tiens,'* she muttered. Like poor Yorick, she had sustained a hit, a very palpable hit. She hadn't bargained for a riposte with such profound semiotic dimensions. Was there perhaps a threat that my aunt might be about to take a hand in the affair, or perhaps even that she was an official from the dreaded fisc, God forbid? She crumpled, her girth suddenly and magically shrunk; disoriented, she crossed herself and sought refuge in the dark recesses of her office. A white puff of smoke went up from the chimney outside. Victory was mine. Bless you, Henri Smith, the countless times you used to call me 'imbecile' and hurl the chalk at me were not in vain.

With a French P45 staring her in the face, Mlle Piaf returned to the counter and with ill grace bade me complete a *fiche*, muttering the while that I might have to vacate the room next day. Presumably, when President Mitterand turned up. Then she retired once again to her little compound.

I now turned to the remaining items on my agenda. First, I must inspect the plumbing in the room to assess the adjustments needed; I carry a small tool kit and a plumb-it-yourself manual for this. In the event, the cistern flushed beautifully as I entered the lavatory with a roar slightly less shattering than the Big Drop at Victoria Falls. The trouble was that I hadn't yet pulled the handle. My first thought was that the opening of the door had triggered the cistern flushing mechanism but a test disproved the theory. It emerged that when the occupant of the room next door with facilities backing on to mine pulled his handle, he flushed not only his own toilet but mine as well. I judged this interesting example of Gallic economy as admirable, but foresaw obvious inconveniences.

Unhappily, it was at this juncture that the valve decided to stick so that the flushing continued unchecked. I reached for my stilson, spanners and pliers and went to work on the cistern. Sadly, there was no cistern to be seen. It was only after removal of a plate that seemed to be fastened terminally to the back wall that I uncovered a Byzantine agglomeration of a kind of ballcock with some wheels and levers that must have been installed about the time of Borodino. The hydrostatic plan would have defeated Galileo himself. I managed to staunch the flushing and, praise heaven, the flow came reluctantly and haltingly to a stop. By this time the pan was clogged with the debris that always seems to attend any plumbing operation I engage in, but there was no sign of a brush with which to clear it. I have noticed before that the French do not recognize the existence of the common lavatory brush. I was minded of the story of the bucolic visitor who bought one at the Ideal Home Exhibition. When asked by his friend, 'How are you getting on with it?' 'Oh, not too good, we're back on paper again,' was Murphy's reply.

This done, my next task is usually to check the television and adjust it to a half-watchable state; more than that I would not hope for. Unless you are a fan of the unending succession of dog-food commercials, the truth is that French TV programmes are so execrable that I now complain if the set *is* working. I am not in favour of violence on television, unless it is directed against those responsible for the dishonest timetables and the uninspired, puerility of the fare offered. Nevertheless, on principle, I examined it. It turned out to be a cable rental job and a large red notice featuring a skull and crossbones warned me not to remove the back on pain of death by about 10,000 volts or worse. The danger of 10,000 volts up my system was definitely not justified by the entertainment in view so I settled for a dark picture where I could discern with much squinting the faint outlines of movement accompanied by raised voices and hysterical laughter from a cretinous studio audience. I deduced that it was one of those provincial French comedic games that culminated with the revelation (to no one's surprise) that the principal female lead had whipped off her wig and was unmasked as a female impersonator in drag.

The last of my preliminary surveys is to confirm that the connecting door with the next room is locked and is stout enough to baffle the sound of a television at full blast, a yapping Pekingese and/or a first-class fight between husband and wife before retiring and snoring the night through like sex-starved buffaloes, while decent people are trying to sleep. In this instance, I found that the insulation wasn't even near to adequate but there was nothing I could do; I decided that if the noise in the night became unbearable and I rejected suicide as an avenue of escape, I would have to have recourse to the fist and the old wall-thumping and shouting routine.

To complete my initial investigation, I checked the tariff card displayed by ministerial ukase on the door and was not surprised to find that the room rate advertised there was at high season level although that stage was not due for another three weeks. A showdown with Ms Piaf later led to a promise of correction but of course nothing was changed and the bill presented when I left, demanded the higher rate.

When I came to deal with secondary formalities like changing up some money (where I found the special cupidity rate offered by the management was two francs less than the official sterling rate) and requesting that the reception desk be sure to pass on some important telephone messages I was expecting, there was a flood of apathy at the counter. Ms Piaf made it abundantly clear that that transmission of telephone messages was a service that not even Prince Louis Napoleon himself could command and told me in French, 'Pas bloody likely'. I was also going to have to submit to the exchange rate scam but I wasn't happy about it. It wasn't the money, it was the principle of the thing. After all, I don't need the money – I have enough money to last me the rest of my life. Unless, of course, I want to buy something.

I resolved to take dinner and an early night. I had checked out the lift which clearly dated from the period before lifts were invented. It had a mind of its own. In the usual way, the light comes on when you step into it; in this one, after attention by the joker laughingly called the maintenance engineer (he also doubled as the night porter), the light went out as you crossed the threshold and came on again when you departed. I elected to use the five flights of stairs to descend to the lobby en route to a nearby bistro where I began at last to relax under the influence of a large *digestif*. I tucked into a Lucullan meal, marred only by the copious clouds of smoke emanating from a neanderthal mountain of a man at the next table, chain-puffing a series of nauseous black cheroots. M Neanderthal weighed in at about 20 stone of muscle, gut and flab; with his napkin tucked into a fold in his neck and a litre of Estandon in his massive fist, he devoted himself to the serious consumption of a gargantuan meal to the accompaniment of much random rumbling, tooth-sucking and lip-smacking. I considered a politely phrased request to ask him to desist from blowing his foul smoke over my way but after reconsideration decided against it because I didn't want my face smashed in.

I called for the bill and that was my second shock. In my tiredness, I had neglected to study the menu prices, most of which I now perceived to be marked 'SC'. I was therefore not prepared for an account that was about three times steeper than I'd bargained for. Perhaps the cashier thought I was Prince Louis Napoleon. I did just scrape together enough to pay it but had nothing left with which to tip the waiter. I recalled that in a similar predicament Proust asked the waiter to lend him 20 francs. The waiter said, 'Of course, M'sieu,' and produced a note from his pocket. 'No, no, you keep it,' said Proust, 'it was for you anyway.' I compromised by giving a puzzled waiter a collection of English, French and Dutch coins instead.

The Cote d'Azur was suffering a cold spell and when I returned to my room, it was apparent that it had no means of heating other than the air-conditioning which had long since expired. I considered the old traveller's trick of turning on the hot tap in the shower room and leaving its door open but I refrained, remembering Woody Allen's story of the time he tried this ploy in a New York hotel. Billows of steam coming into the room met the cold air front seeping under the window sill with the result that it started to rain in the room.

I climbed into bed, exhausted, praying for a peaceful night, but it was not to be. As I'd puffed up the stairs, I'd noticed my neighbours emerging from the antediluvian lift and disappearing into Room 512 next door. He was an old man, slow in gait with laboured breathing, eighty years of age or more. His companion was much younger, thirtyish, shrill, heavily rouged and bright-eyed, decorated with dangling gypsy earrings and a minuscule skirt that could have done as a pelmet in a very small apartment. Her shapely legs were planted in gold shoes with four inch heels. She cooed and fondled the inevitable poodle to her ample bosom as she flounced in.

 I drifted into an uneasy sleep to the sound of clinking glasses and high-pitched giggling and awoke at midnight to an assault on my ears that was far more offensive than my worst fears – it was like VE Day all over again. The giggling continued but was now interspersed with grunting, presumably from the old man, and yapping, presumably from the poodle (although I would not swear to this). I dared not speculate what part the dog played in the scenario. There was much creaking of furniture and the walls did nothing to contain the sounds – indeed, they might just as well have been frolicking in my room. My thumping on the common wall was lost in the welter of noise that had attained the fury of the artillery duel at El Alamein. I became seriously alarmed when my centre hanging light fitting began to swing violently. They may have been practising trampolining but I don't think so. It occurred to me that the old chap must have discovered a new Kama Sutra position – doing it with one foot in the grave; he must have had a pair of jump leads. I only hoped it hadn't been too much for him. The all-night round of stomping and scampering continued through the small hours until at about four in the morning, just as I had fallen into fitful unconsciousness, there was a thunderous crash as if the ceiling had fallen in. I speculated that justice had prevailed and my neighbours lay pinned helpless under the furniture. There was no such relief, however, for the hubbub soon resumed and only petered out as dawn broke. There then began a sequence of Bashan-type snoring fit to wake the dead; the walls shuddered. The new visitation was supported by regular yapping (from the poodle?).

I heard them preparing to leave at about seven o'clock and as much in curiosity as in indignation, I hurried into the corridor to confront them. I was amazed at the scene I beheld. The old gent was now erect, springy of step and seemingly twenty years younger for his exertions. He wore a self-satisfied expression with the smile of one who has caught a glimpse of heaven, has seen a vision of greatness before it was too late. On the other hand, the girlfriend who had danced merrily in a few hours before now tottered out, minus one earring, rickety on her feet and with hand pressed to her lumbar region. She looked awful. It is uncharitable to rejoice at other people's misfortunes but I could scarce forebear to reflect on that old tag about just desserts. So, I re-entered my room. By the way, I noticed that the pooch was stiff and silent as it limped after them.

I fell into bed at 7.15 and lost consciousness at once. At 7.30, after a perfunctory tap on the door, a waiter walked in with a tray of continental breakfast and a chit for me to sign. Through the blur of sleep-starved eyes, I saw that the chit read 411, not 511, and I exploded. The waiter was startled as an apparently demented Englishman leaped from his bed and, knife in hand, quite naked, chased him out of the room to take refuge in the fifth floor pantry. '*Il est fou, cet homme de cinq cents onze, n'est ce pas*?' he gasped at the chambermaid.

Thus ended the first 24 hours of my French vacation. The one consolation was that things could only get better.

Next year, Bognor Regis?

15

WHAT'S IN A NAME – AND WHO CARES?

As the man on the Clapham omnibus once observed so shrewdly to me, while musing on the rich tapestry of life in the Brixton Road, onomatology can be eximious. Saying which, he rose and got off hurriedly as the conductor came to collect his fare. Had he lingered, he would have further informed me that name dubbing starts in school. In fact, it is very many years since I trod those hallowed Owen's halls. The actuarial pundits aver that with advance in medical science our life expectancy has been extended. Nevertheless, there are incredulous people about who express disbelief and even amazement when they learn that I'm still alive. The truth is that the delay is only because I'm still looking for a loophole in St Paul's admonition to Timothy – 'We brought nothing into this world and we carry nothing out.' Anyway, I'm not all that ancient; after all, Lloyd George knew my father. So, if it has no other purpose, the appearance of this essay carrying my authorship serves as a reminder that I'm still around.

Harking back to the dim distant Islington days, I can only recall one occasion when I was 'named' and achieved at the same time what might be described as the 15 minutes of fame to which Andy Warhol claimed everyone is entitled. It happened in this way.

I was not noted for academic brilliance. I worked on what was known as the 'stopped clock' plan, namely that to be bright all the time was to be too clever by half and that it was enough to rely on the Turkish proverb that says that even a stopped clock is right twice a day. I was fifteen and my friend Dick Simpson, a rakish late developer, was eighteen. He moved in boxing circles and was a member of Lane's Club in Baker Street, where aspiring young wrestlers were welcome to practise in the ring. I was a devoted fan and accompanied Dick on his visits there, thrilled to rub shoulders with famous names of the wrestling world. I learned some of the skills of the all-in sport in my quest for the fine-tuned sinewy physique I was later to boast. (No abusive letters from dressing-room neighbours, please.)

My speciality was the flying arm take-over, an over the shoulder throw that I had tried out in our horsing about activity in the gym. After all, I reasoned, what was the point of acquiring the skills if you didn't use them? Thus it was that on the occasion in question, the plan was for me, stripped for action, to wait behind the gym door during a morning break and on a signal from a lookout that a studious, mild-mannered boy we called Louis von Gatt was about to enter, I was to haul him in and hurl him forward over my shoulder in a flying take-over onto a mat set in place to receive him. The plan worked perfectly save for one small detail, it was not Louis but languages master 'Jimmy' Cracknell who entered, on his way to visit his colleague PT 'Taffy' Lloyd. Cracknell was a small wiry man, decent enough but with a short fuse at the best of times and was easily ruffled by pressures of this kind. I think it is not overstating the case to say that he was somewhat surprised and disappointed as he sailed through the air to land on the mat with a resounding thump. When he recovered his breath, he seemed unable to accept what was after all only a reasonable mistake and, as I explained, one that anyone could make. In fact, he twitched and fulminated and became so agitated that we feared he had suffered brain damage; in his exasperation, he actually lost control of his tongue and babbled like a tuba player set to play Rimsky-Korsakov's *Flight of the Bumble Bee.*

I was not the apple of Cracknell's eye before the incident; a tenuous teacher/pupil relationship had hitherto been of the Dotheboys Hall variety. I wasn't anarchic and Cracknell wasn't tyrannous but I confess I was too easily diverted to the jokey in his lessons and while I was supposedly immersed in the conjugation of French verbs, the temptation to toss Doug Young's cap out of the third-floor window to the street below was too great. Cracknell prayed to a merciful God to take me away to the next phase of my career, likely in his estimation to be as a washer-up in a Kings Cross doss-house, so that he could resume a tranquil journey towards pension time. Accordingly, his fund of patience was spent and as soon as he could articulate he spat out an epithet coupled with an expletive that certainly had never before been delivered in anger in a grammar school gym (at any rate, by a respected languages master of mature years). I could imagine the headline in the *News of the World*, 'Schoolmaster Attacked by Crazed Half-Naked Pupil' with me disgraced and walking into the sunset as my school career came to a premature end. Fortunately, Cracknell cooled down and I was spared a visit to the Head's study. Instead, he gave me the opportunity of further airing my wrestling skills, this time with a massive impot in detention. The reverberations died down after a while but the epithet, unsuitable for printing here, was to stick to me disagreeably for some time.

Up to this time, I had never been bothered by being renamed, even when my parents' matrimonial record was put in doubt. True, at one time it was the absence rather than the conferment of a name that caused me to feel slightly second class; when coming to Owen's School at the age of ten, I found that almost everyone else had at least two first names whereas my parents had only given me one and I had no middle initial. I cured this hiatus by inventing one and became Sidney S for a while but I soon tired of the pretence and the complications it caused and turned my attention to preoccupations more important to my school progress, like cricket, snooker and girls. Not necessarily in that order.

When my fellows noted that my name was very like that of the popular brand of liver salts, I acquired the name Kruschen. When we progressed later on to French lessons and they learned that the French for pig was *cochon*, they again spotted the likeness to my name and my appellation was formally revised to Cochon. I was far from offended for it was a mark of distinction to be given a nickname. To be called by your real name was a sign that you had not been admitted to the inner circle. I was proud to be accepted as an insider. The Cracknell designation was of another sort, grubby and excessively vicious.

A large plump chap named Watson was of course called 'Fatty' and a classmate with a slender girlish figure, who had a propensity for blushing when addressed, was cruelly called 'Nancy'. Many years later, after distinguished war service overseas, he confided that his mother had dressed him as a girl until he was ten. I am still in touch with another former pupil, one of the school's great sporting achievers, who was nicknamed 'Black Rod' and is still so known. I am in no position to disclose the genesis of the title.

The teaching staff were not exempt from the name embellishments. Head Master Revd HN Asman became 'Taz' (rhyming), 'Flash Pete' Hardwick (elegance of manner and dress), 'Pussy' Heath (stealthy approach), 'Pop' Dixon (son in VIth form), 'Beaky' Shaw (proboscis), and 'Soap' Grant (origin unknown) were typical examples. In the world at large, we find some quaint cases of name-changing. Luciano Pavarotti has become 'Fat Lucy', Lord Bottomley 'Bumley' and Sir Hartley Shawcross MP, thought to have switched political allegiance, became Sir Shortly Floorcross. A female marketing guru in New York only recently reported that when she changed her name from Faith Plotkin to Faith Popcorn, her career took off. I find that Michael Jackson is known in America as Wacko Jacko. In the eponymy category, Thomas Crapper is, truly, the firm that makes lavatory fittings.

Now that obituary tributes in the press are becoming less hagiographic, curious details of name adoptions surface. A notice in the *Liverpool Echo* not long ago informed readers of the death of Takashima Yamaguchi, a prominent resident of the city and a member of a distinguished Japanese family. Mr Yamaguchi had been resident in Liverpool for so long, so the report ran, that he was regarded as a scouse. It went on, 'Mr Yamaguchi was a close relative of Emperor Hirohito but was known to all his friends as Paddy Murphy.'

An unintentional conversion was reported by David Profumo of the time a haberdasher named Williams approached Teddy Roosevelt in a crowd and shook him by the hand. 'Mr President,' he said, 'I made your shirts.' 'Oh yes,' came the reply, 'I remember you well, Major Shurtz.'

By the way, I have been unable to verify that a shorter handle was assumed by a man named Twisleton-Wykeham-Fiennes, but I have traced a man who has changed his name by deed pool to Zebedee Zzzzzzzy in order to be the last name in the telephone directory. I am also investigating the story that Robert Maxwell is alive and is now known as Bert Higgins, working as a plumber's mate in Walthamstow. And bad news, Miss Snuggle Bottom who always sends you a Valentine's card is not a cover for the boss's nubile, mini-skirted secretary, but is the flirty tea lady.

You may well ask at this point if it really matters and if a nickname or a name change is worth noticing at all. Surely the man on the Clapham omnibus doesn't give a fig what name is conferred on him. So let us turn at this juncture to eminent authorities who have gone public on the question. What, the sage from Clapham asks, do William Shakespeare, King Edward VII and Mrs Florrie Impleton have in common? The answer is that these three learned authorities have all studied the issue and have had the percipience to promulgate their conclusion, namely that none has any time for diverse or pretentious styles of name or title. First, we have Shakespeare, of whom some of the more literate among you may have heard, one who has proved himself no slouch when it comes to applied logic. Will made plain his indifference to the ascription of names when he penned the immortal lines, 'What's in a name? That which we call a rose by any other name would smell as sweet.' (At any rate, someone penned it – if it wasn't him, it was Bacon.) Good enough, isn't it?

Enter Florrie Impleton, of whom you may not have heard. She has good credentials. When I was a boy and living in Tufnell Park, the said Mrs Florrie Impleton was our daily help; she would sail heroically down Holloway Road twice weekly, come slush, rain or shine, to help my mother with the housework. She was a stout, hard-working soul with Amazon-like upper arms and a pudgy mud-coloured face onto which there dangled heavy drop earrings. Never fazed, a rock of reliability, she became an honorary member of our family. She supported an out-of-work husband, four hulking sons and the tavern on the corner of Rupert Road. I don't know if she's alive still, but if she is she'd be 122 now. However, for some reason now unclear, the name Impleton always seemed to me in my unworldly innocence a great joke, perhaps because it seemed a pantomime name, perhaps with a Simple Simon connection. Whatever the reason, my elder brother gave me a stern warning to mind my manners unless I was looking for a thick ear. I was not seeking any alteration to my aural equipment so asked Florrie what she would like me to call her. And here she demonstrated the candour, wit and wisdom that combined to make her a figure of authority. Her response was as quick as a flash as she snapped back, 'I don't mind what you call me as long as you don't call me too late for me dinner.'

Some cynics allege that she must have been a student

of the Bard's (or Bacon's) work and had only borrowed his stance after reading *Romeo and Juliet* but frankly, I doubt it; that theory is about as likely as her uncorking a bottle of Dom Perignon for tea. No, she made her case independently and unequivocally after a period of profound study, a comprehensive declaration of her disinterestedness in whatever agnomen we might give her. In so doing, she put her imprimatur on the manifesto already adduced by her distinguished colleague Will Shakespeare (or Bacon).

I would have added the name of Gertrude Stein ('Rose is a rose is a rose') to the panel of eminent authorities but as she died in 1946 and was cremated, I found it difficult to make contact with her.

In the light of the powerful testimony I have presented, I submit that the case for complete licence in the use of names is proved. However, a note of caution should be sounded for it is wise to exercise restraint in the use of substitute monikers. An incident on a recent visit to Glasgow taught me the need to be selective. Some know-all had told me a *booba-maiseh* that if wishing to ingratiate yourself with a stranger in Scotland, all you have to do is use 'Jock' as a form of address. Accordingly, following this advice, I approached an erect, ruddy-faced chap outside the station; he seemed a civilized empathic sort and proffering my hand, I observed cordially, 'Hello, Jock, nice day.' He looked at it as if I had yellow fever. The word 'Jock' was like a red rag to a bull and Dr Jekyll became Mr Hyde at a stroke. He juxtaposed just two monosyllabic words, one of four and the other of three letters, stepped into a car at the kerb-side and drove deliberately onto the pavement with the clear aim of running me down. As I leaped out of the way, the realization dawned on me that the over-familiarity of a nickname could be offensive and must only be used with discretion. I wasn't to know that he was a crusty ex-Brigade of Guards officer up from Cheltenham for the day, and that his surname was Strapp, was I? So, be wary, if you pick the wrong man you might find yourself given a new name you won't relish; there's an old Yiddish curse that runs, 'May you become famous, may they name a disease after you.'

Oh yes, you are wondering how the third member, King Edward VII, earned inclusion in the distinguished triumvirate of expert authorities. I can disclose that he put on record his denial of the importance of titles when, on board a yacht, he was heard by the cabin steward to cry, irritably, 'Put another cushion under your back and for God's sake, stop calling me sir!'

16

POVERTY IS NO CRIME BUT IT'S BETTER TO BE RICH THAN POOR

In these hard times when we alumni no longer breakfast on plover's eggs, smoked salmon and champagne, we can be excused for attitudes that are primarily material. There's an old German proverb that goes, 'The uncle who brings the ham is superior to the aunt who plays the piano.'

There is a story of a successful English entrepreneur who flew out to Zurich to call on the manager of one of the big Swiss banks. He was ushered into a vast panelled room resplendent with period furniture and works of art. 'I'd like to open a numbered account,' he began, a little nervously. 'How much do you have in mind to deposit, sir?' asked the manager. Our man pushed a bag towards him and whispered, 'Two million pounds.' 'There's no need to whisper, sir,' came the response, 'poverty is no crime.'

No, poverty may not be a crime but at the same time, it's never particularly welcome, especially in the present straitened climate. I am no hedonist, but I have no wish to end my days conducting my business affairs and writing these essays starving in the cramped quarters of a cardboard box on the Embankment. Thus it is that I have been driven to consider ways of conserving my capital.

We need feel no shame about being cost-conscious these days, but with the benefit of hindsight, some of our actions can be less than sensible; in fact, they just go to show how idiotic one can be. For instance, I do now see that to have asked the local Sumo-type greengrocer for a discount on a bag of potatoes was thoughtless and warranted the riposte that I might like a punch up the throat. On Monday of last week however, I must have suffered a brainstorm because no rational man of long matrimonial standing would have done what I did. True, these are hard times and I was looking about me for potential economies in the household budget, but really it was an error of judgement to suggest McDonald's for a celebration supper on the wife's birthday and it was equally unwise to send her last year's birthday card with the date (quite clearly I thought) tippexed out. But I should have been declared insane before launching the pay phone project. My eye had lighted on an item displayed in the Sunday newspaper bargain columns. A pay phone in the house. A brilliant idea, I thought, just the thing to cut down on excessively lengthy telephone conversations between you-know-who and her relatives.

Of course, you, who are so much wiser and worldlier than me, will already be smiling sadly, wondering at my naïvety and will experience no surprise whatever at the ensuing drama. I brought the instrument home but formal installation was never achieved. My beloved saw me with tools in hand and enquired, already a little frostily, what I was doing. I told her I was exchanging our traditional phone for a pay phone. There was a short pause while she gathered her powers of speech. She then explained courteously her opinion of the project and made the point that it seemed to her no less than a gratuitous insult to her family and especially to her dressmaker. She proceeded to empty a saucepan of spaghetti bolognese over my head in order to make her position quite clear. I wouldn't have minded so much but she knows I like parmesan cheese with my bolognese. Then she threw me out into the street with the new pay phone coiled around my ears. The doctor will be telling me later if my arm is broken. Love–15.

When I was at school, my contemporaries always thought I was the chap most likely to marry outside his species. This has been proved accurate because Mrs K is a perfectly normal human being. This being so, it was only natural that my attempts at economizing on the household grocery bills have not met with universal approval. I insisted on some cuts in the expenditure on provisions; however, after only a few weeks of the new order, I found I had to call at the doctor complaining of weakness. He listened to the account of my symptoms and asked for some details of my eating habits. After a sharp intake of breath and a retreat to the safety of the other side of his desk, he muttered something about malnutrition and pronounced that the dietary regime I had adopted invariably leads to scurvy and rickets. A nervous twitch, he added, comes later on. I returned home and conveyed this news to Mrs K, whereupon she went into immediate action by raising the weekly housekeeping allowance collectible from me to a level that was 10% higher than it had been before I began my ill-starred campaign. Love–30.

It was only last weekend that she'd expressed doubts about my attempts at economy when the vacuum cleaner ceased to work. I assured her that apart from the adventure and self-satisfaction involved, here was a golden opportunity to do a simple job myself rather than call in the local electrical repairer to put the damned thing right (minimum call-out charge £30). She put her coat on and left for a place of safety while the repair operation was in process. How prescient she was. Before she went, she left me instructions for calling the fire brigade.

As I write, looking at me on the floor is a bag, some cable, a heap of machinery and sundry nuts, bolts and screws. Oh yes, and Volume One of *Newton's Mechanics*. Later on today, I must go along to John Lewis for a new vacuum cleaner and then call on the doctor for treatment for burns sustained on passing 240 volts of electric power supply through my right arm. I'll get the electrician to locate and replace the fuses I've blown. Unless, of course, he's flown down to his villa in the South of France. Love–40.

Like you, my favourite target for economy is any expenditure which gives no tangible value in return. High on my list in this category is car-parking penalties. These disbursements give no recompense or satisfaction of any kind. There can be few experiences left that afford more innocent and unheralded joy than the thrill of finding two hours unexpired time on a meter. I shudder and feel physical revulsion when I see a vehicle being loaded spitefully onto a truck for transportation to the pound or with an ugly clamp attached to a wheel. These methods of enforcement in the name of unobstructed passage on our roads seem to me nasty, oppressive and unEnglish and one day I shall be appearing on a charge of breach of the peace as I handcuff myself to the wheels of a car being so mistreated. I wonder how long it will be before wardens are authorized, nay ordered, to leap out into the road and yank drivers out of their cars on the move and affix tickets to the windscreens. And confiscate the vehicles if immediate payment is not forthcoming. For that matter, will it be long before non-drivers are picked up on the pavement and arrested for not wearing seat-belts?

Then there are the butcher's bills. Frankly I've had my eye on the scraps kept for the dog, not only because there's a potential saving there but because he's eating far better than I am. The fact is that when she's shopping at the butcher, I have to admit that the wife insists on having the best cuts. Not for me, but for him. The trouble is that she's spotted my special interest in his menu and now keeps his dinner locked away in a cupboard. Dogs are shrewd and intuitive, you know, and our animal – Charlie by name – has begun to avoid me. While I'm cutting corners with some scrag-end of lamb left over from last week, the sight of him slopping away at a dish of finest minced beef, blissfully uninterested in the sacrifice that has made it possible, is hard to bear and I can't help growling at him. I know just how a lamppost feels about dogs. He knows full well I'd like to give him his P45. When he does look at me, I swear he sneers.

No, the means of survival seem to lie in a choice between reducing costs or increase of income. As to the latter, I have been cogitating. In the eighteenth century, ministers and judges openly took bribes. In certain parts of America, the practice is still unashamedly pursued. I was myself asked recently in California by a friend who is a member of the Senate if I get much in the way of 'kickbacks'; when I protested that the idea was unthinkable, it was clear that I fell several rungs in his esteem and he walked off and didn't even wish me a nice day. But I wonder if it's worth moving to the LA bench?

As for saving in energy, I recall Gracie Allen's classic advice for not overdoing roast beef: 'Take one large roast beef and one small roast beef,' she said. 'Put them in the oven. When the little one burns, the big one is done.' No, there's no scope for saving there.

The sad fact is that the spectre of escalating costs outweighs our feeble stratagems. I think I'll abandon my plans for repairing my own shoes, buying my next suit from Oxfam and making home-made wine for special celebrations, and let the pennies fall where they may. After all, like steroids, we may cure one mischief only to be faced with some even more unwelcome side-effect. I have reached this conclusion after a comprehensive rebuff to my campaign. If persisted with, my matrimonial condition could be brought into jeopardy so that I prefer to run up the white flag and admit defeat. For example, I do not consider that my suggestion was so preposterous or bizarre but it was not well received. I merely reminded my wife of the old adage that drink is the curse of the working classes and that there might be scope for saving by cutting out gin. It may have been unwise. Game, set and bloody match.

17

THE SHOCKING CASE OF THE KOREAN SWORDFISH

I really have to complain. We live in desperately hard times and given an outstanding record of invention and innovation, I must confess to surprise and disappointment that I have not been summoned to No. 10 to unveil a solution to present economic problems. Regrettably and inexplicably, I do not enjoy recognition by those in charge. I note sadly that my parents named me 'Samuel', my friends call me 'Sam' but the cashier at the bank still calls me 'Next'.

Although official credit has been denied me, I can disclose with what is, I hope, modest pride that I have been at the sharp end in many world events in my time including, to name but a few, the development of the atom bomb, the radar system and the discovery of penicillin. Alexander Fleming was my next-door neighbour at Highgate and was in fact under my direction when he discovered the life-saving drug; it was indeed from me that he borrowed the cheese that went mouldy. And where do you think Mike Gatting got that reverse sweep from? Who do you think inspired the giant Arsenal mural? Whose key unlocked the mystery of crop circles? And who writes Frank Bruno's speeches? *Res ipsa loquitur.* Yet, I have not been called.

I suggest very strongly that inventors are treated with suspicion in this country – you know, the old 'too clever by half' Macleod slur. Anyone coming up with a fresh idea is about as popular here as Jacques Delors at a British Legion reunion. Frankly, I think it's time for a change, for the establishment of a Ministry for the Encouragement of New Ideas to lift the country out of its trough. Many and varied are the unsung heroes who would step into the breach. Just consider some of the unknowns who have already earned Britain honour and prosperity.

Take Joseph Moorhouse. I met him in the 1950s after he had become friendly with our daily help and had proposed marriage. They had seen the priest with a view to publishing the banns but after hearing of Joseph's background, he had privately counselled Nora to think again and she had consulted me. I invited Joseph to call and that is how I came to hear of his remarkable exploits. He first explained that he was just returned from the Korean campaign where he'd been awarded the Victoria Cross. I pressed him and he modestly revealed that it was thanks to the invention for which he'd won his decoration that Allied submarines were able to operate in the Far East freely and without interference. He had devised a corridor that could be extruded between two submersibles under water and side by side, to enable the safe transference of men and supplies from one to the other. This, he explained, had revolutionized the effectiveness of submarine warfare. He paused and then added, 'There was only one danger. Nervously, I asked what that was. 'Swordfish,' he replied succinctly and dramatically. 'The corridor was vulnerable to attack by swordfish, perhaps enemy trained; I soon solved that by fitting electric shock wiring to the outer skin of the passage.' A fantastic tale of resource, almost unbelievable, was it not? He disclosed to me in confidence that even as we spoke he was engaged on another highly secret operation for MI5 and gave me a telephone number to contact a Colonel Carruthers for a reference and confirmation of his status. I called the number which rather to my surprise turned out to be that of the Arlington House men's hostel at Camden Town, but on reflection I thought an admirable place for a secret branch of MI5. Yes, they had a Joseph Moorhouse staying there nightly but no, they knew of no Colonel Carruthers.

It all seemed quite bizarre but you know how eccentric inventors are and as we have ever learned, truth is stranger than fiction. With ruddy face part-covered by a straggly red beard, a thick striped three-piece suit, brown boots and a rubber-dubber trilby hat, Joseph looked unlike a secret agent but I reasoned that this was deliberate to put counter-agents off the scent. On further questioning as to his antecedents, he claimed that he was a member of the well-known Moorhouse Jams family and came from Oblingdon in Lancs. I only got the name Oblingdon after he'd made three attempts at it and I never managed to trace it on the map.

Here, then, you have the paradox of a man noetically simple but capable of discerning a fine concept. Such a man was Percy Shaw, also a Lancastrian, who conceived the brilliant idea of the Cat's-eye, a much-lauded contribution to road safety. The notion came to Shaw as he was walking along the street one evening and noted a cat coming towards him; he was struck by the startling luminescence of the animal's eyes and set to work to invent the Cat's-eye for the roads of the world, making a fortune while so doing. But consider, what a lucky thing it was that the cat was walking towards him, not going away, otherwise he would have invented the pencil sharpener.

It is curious but true that members of the theatrical profession are reputed to have a special fund of resourcefulness for improvisation and fresh ideas. Actors are rarely at a loss when faced with the unexpected. A leading actor in a bedroom drama is recently reported in such a situation, when the telephone rings at a crucial point in the action but when he goes to answer it, he cannot because there isn't one; the stage manager has tripped over it and trodden on it. With only a moment's hesitation, the actor dives under the bed and continues an imaginary telephone conversation on the lines of the scripted dialogue, albeit rather muffled. As he emerges, he says for the benefit of the audience, 'God knows where that damn maid will put it next.'

I was in the audience at a play where the central character decides to shoot his rival. 'I am going to kill you,' he cried and pointed the pistol and pulled the trigger. Not a sound was heard. He pulled it twice more but still there was no sound of a shot. Nonplussed for only an instant, he charged towards his adversary, shouting, 'Shooting's too good for you, you scum, I'm going to kick you to death,' and proceeded to do so furiously as the curtain came down. Yet another well-documented story is of the quick-witted enterprise of the great Shakespearean actor William Macready in *Macbeth*; after his soliloquy he bounded into the wings where his dresser was always waiting with a bucket of stage blood in which the actor would dip his hands before going back on to announce his murder of Duncan. One evening, he did this but the dresser was nowhere to be found so Macready punched a stage-hand in the nose, held his hands under his bleeding nostrils and raced back on stage to inform Lady M, 'I have done the deed, didst thou not hear the noise?'

A combination of ingenuity and wisdom is illustrated in the tale of the property developer who recently came home to his wife after a traumatic session with his accountant and told her, 'We have to economize. You read a cookery book and we'll sack the chef.' She thought for a minute and said, 'I've got a better idea. You read the *Kama Sutra* and we'll sack the gardener.'

While applauding innovators with ideas it would be idle not to concede that some of these pathfinders lose their balance. The other evening I had the misfortune while representing Old Owen's at a cricket dinner to be seated next to the president of another North London club, a successful local tradesman and a generous supporter, but as a member of the human race a throw-back to the Pliocene era. Never have teeth been so gritted. Mr

Windbag purported to have the solution to all our current problems, especially that of umpiring disputes and dissent by footballers and cricketers on the field, a subject of serious concern in sporting circles. He hinted that he was already working with the TCCB on a plan and adduced a string of arguments, all of them jejune. In essence, it seemed that he was advocating forcible removal to a police cell for offending players. He debouched a flog'em and hang'em manifesto while including some crude anecdotes at which he would cackle deafeningly so as to drown out any opposition that might come from another part of the table. My guess is that he'd never in his life been nearer to Lord's than a Camden Town off-licence and knew as much about cricket as I do about the sex life of the badger. Table manners hadn't figured large in his curriculum and peas sped all over the table as he alternated between balancing them on his knife and trying to spear them with his fork. Debris from an overfull orifice showered his neighbours as he orated and coated his salmon en croute liberally with salt and vinegar.

At last, the formal toasts began and he boomed, 'But let's count our blessings, friends, and don't be downhearted, eh?' Old Owenians, show me a pompous ass who thus closes his peroration and I'll show you a man with a large index-linked pension.

Having reached the end of my essay, I note that it has been accomplished once again without recourse to politics, religion, four-letter words, sex or violence – not a bad record these days. There can be no carping by allegations of salty or naughty allusions. In this connection, may I call on and paraphrase Dr Johnson who, in response to a lady who complained of naughty words in his dictionary, said, 'Madam, you must have had great fun looking them up.' He was a wise old bird, was that Sam Johnson; he it was who observed, 'No man but a blockhead ever wrote, except for money,' I wouldn't be surprised to learn that some part of his education was spent at Owen's School.

18

A NOSE BY ANY OTHER NAME

Whatever your line of country, there is generally a lighter side that surfaces from time to time, isn't there? For instance, I'm told by a colleague whose travels frequently take him to Japan that there is a notice in a Tokyo bar reading, 'Special cocktails for ladies with nuts'. In my own case, as I reflect on my time on the bench, I perceive that the courts of justice are especially fecund as a source of interesting stories, perhaps because in many ways the courts are foci of the current social condition. Some of the tales that are told are authentic gems but others are possibly as apocryphal as they are whimsical, a godsend for music-hall comedians. One such is of the defendant found guilty of deception, having affixed Green Shield trading stamps instead of the authorized National Insurance variety all over his insurance card. The chairman of the magistrates, after a bibulous lunch, is said to have commented, 'This is a bad case of dishonesty; I'm going to give you six months – and an electric kettle.' Another was of the court-house keeper who discovered that a toilet seat had gone missing and informed the local press that the police had not yet apprehended the culprit, 'because they had nothing to go on'.

In the authentic category, we have a wealth of stories on official record. It was only recently that a bench chairman interrupted the sentencing of a defendant to order the defence solicitor to leave court because his shoelaces were undone.

It was in the domestic proceedings court that I recall a disillusioned husband, a writer, sarcastically quoting Brendan Behan with the plea, 'Why does any woman give herself the trouble that husbands are when with less trouble she could buy and train a cat?' And equally poignant but reasonable was the evidence given by another husband whose wife, a Mrs Bertha Gass, complained that he hadn't spoken to her for three years. Cross-examined, he was asked if this was true. 'Yes,' he admitted, sadly, 'I didn't want to interrupt her.'

To illustrate the theme of this essay to which, if you are patient I shall eventually come, let me recount a tragic case with which I was once concerned in the Crown Court. The facts are that a gentleman attends a 'spots and stripes' party at a house in Palmers Green (for the uninitiated I should explain that this was a party where gay guests dressed in spotted wear and the others wore striped garments, a fact which I uncovered after I had made a point of displaying judicial ignorance). The court is asked by the appellant to allow an appeal against a disqualification from driving imposed by the lower court for excess alcohol and in support submits that there were 'special circumstances'.

The circumstances adduced are indeed special in that after consumption of copious quantities of lager and Babycham, a Stripe has taken against a Spot and, in a fracas, has bitten off a part of the latter's nose. Although as spaced as a newt, Stripes puts Spots into his car and gets him erratically but safely to the North Middlesex Hospital where a doctor informs him that if he can produce the missing piece of the proboscis they may be able to stitch it back but that immediate action is of the essence. Failing that Spot's nose will be an ex-nose.

Stripes climbs back into the car with the stricken Spots and speeds off to the site of the party but, inevitably, the fates take a hand and he is stopped and breathalysed. In due course, he appears before the magistrates and is fined heavily and disqualified from driving. He now appeals to the superior court against the disqualification on the ground that his driving was only undertaken in a grave emergency, namely for the purpose of obtaining urgent medical attention for poor Spots, to try to make his nose whole again. Spots forfeits a day's wages (he is a ladies' hairdresser) to come and give evidence in support of Stripes's plea and the court sees a touching homogeneous camaraderie that has blossomed between the two. Far from seeking revenge or starting any form of legal action against his attacker, Spots's only concern is to minimize the punishment meted out to Stripes.

I cite this episode to illustrate my belief that not so long ago there was a less aggressive side to human nature with a greater generosity of spirit and charity to be found in the community. Even where serious injury was involved, the first impulse was for one to help the other rather than to seek redress. It is no longer thus, alas. Disputes were normally settled pacifically whereas the new order seems to demand that we must never let a grievance pass unrequited.

Keen observers of the current scene like yourselves cannot have failed to note press reportage that the cost of the legal aid system to the Exchequer has escalated alarmingly now that the resources of the courts are being taken up with a proliferation of the run-of-the-mill offences and grievances. Out of date is the cynical old tag about the law, like the Ritz, being open to all. One wonders what has happened to provoke your average citizen to such extravagant indulgence so swiftly to demand retribution for any derogation, real or imagined. Gladiatorial invitations to 'come outside' are in short order. Prosecutions are brought and damage suits touched off at the drop of a hat. Seemingly, no slight may go unpunished; the Brit is hungry for reprisals and bent on satisfaction within or without the law. Nothing is more heinous than loss of face (please see under the heading of 'Road Rage, renowned for') and stiff upper lips are out of fashion. I note that cases are pending of parents of young children who have lost teeth suing manufacturers of sweet drinks.

Even in court itself, restraint is in short supply, as was brought home to me uncomfortably in the Tottenham court when I refused bail to a defendant committed for trial on a rape charge. He showed his displeasure by vaulting out of the dock and hurling his shoes at me. Fortunately for me, he missed, but unfortunately for the court clerk, he scored a bull on the side of his head rendering him deaf in the left ear for some two or three weeks.

On the sporting scene, fair play and good losers are out of favour. Although it might have been least expected there, examples of unworthy behaviour surface only too frequently, leading to prosecutions and disciplining of players in cricket, soccer and rugger engagements, sometimes involving damages claims for serious injury, a state of affairs unheard of up to a few years ago. Happily to recall, there was no trouble in refereeing or umpiring in my time at Owen's and it is reassuring to learn that the discipline of controlled motivation and the code of restraint holds in the present day under the firm direction of sports master Ian Breeze and his colleagues. As I remember it, the match official was usually one of the staff and we quickly learned that it didn't pay to question his decision. A plea for reconsideration of a ruling would meet with a sharp order from Dare or Hutchings to 'Get on with it', sometimes (coincidentally?) followed by a period in detention soon after. Newbolt's 'Play up and Play the Game' was the imperative and we got into the habit of doing the job respectful of authority and without jostling for advantage. As Old Owenians, the training served us well and we were able to take inevitable reverses and feelings of injustice without surrendering dignity or independence.

There were a few exceptions. One memorable instance was that of George Goold at a cricket fixture at Broxbourne in the 1950s. George was a fine and talented sportsman, an excellent bat and a wily spin bowler but inclined to be robust in his approach and sometimes on a short fuse. At Broxbourne, he was in full flood until on a half-hearted speculative appeal from an inexperienced member of the home side, he was given out stumped by an even more inexperienced umpire who was feeling thirst pangs and was not anxious to prolong his separation from a pint or two of bitter. Unhappily, he'd picked the wrong victim on whom to inflict a gross misjudgement and I had a sharp sense of impending crisis as George remained at the crease, staring incredulously at the umpire and becoming increasingly purple of countenance. The umpire was a friendly fellow and made the cardinal error of grinning at George whereupon George uttered an oath, one that we had actually heard before from him when displeased, something about self-infliction of a naughty process, and then he flung his bat with great force at the umpire. He hadn't allowed for the wind and missed his target but scored a bull on the opposing skipper who was fielding at square leg. The latter was the local butcher with a considerable girth and flat feet and was not nearly agile enough to move out of harm's way. I estimate that that little affair cost me six jugs and a large dish of humble pie in the bar later to keep the fixture. Fortunately, George had packed his bag and gone home by then, still chuntering imprecations, else my diplomacy would surely have been in vain.

In latter years, the international scene has also suffered. You will recall that England fast bowler Snow allegedly sent Gavaskar spinning in India as he attempted a short run; he then picked up Gavaskar's bat and threw it at him. He was instructed to apologize to the batsman but was dropped for the next Test. Carr, captaining the MCC in Pakistan, went so far as to empty a bucket of water over the umpire in an effort to make a point. It was quite recent that the Duleep Trophy in India ended in anarchy after a bowler assaulted a batsman with a stump. There are lately recorded cases of umpires 'sledging' players, even of tripping bowlers on the way to the crease. Seeing his compatriot caught at the wicket, one umpire rescued him by calling 'no ball' posthumously. Brawls on the football park are commonplace at the most senior level and a professional player has boasted openly in a video on public sale of head-butting, spitting and foul tactics. A few months back, a former rugby international was sentenced to a term of imprisonment for inflicting grievous bodily harm and breaking an opponent's jaw.

I chronicle and lament the growing tendency, indeed a precipitate rush, for instant remedial action where a cool head should counsel moderation. As far back as 400 BC, Diodotus of Athens was realizing and warning against decisions made in haste or anger. What, we may ask, is behind this modern sinister splurge of belligerence? Is it a natural post-war syndrome or attributable to altered diet, world climate changes or what? I think we should be told. Could it be that television 'entertainment', offering its instant solutions, bears a large responsibility? Another question that occurs to me as relevant is this; if our judicial structure eventually passes into the state of subsidiarity (forgive me, dreaded word) to the supremacy of the European Court of Human Rights, as is being presently envisaged and advertised, will we both be able and willing to afford legal aid?

Incidentally, if you are so nosy as to want to know if in the aforementioned spots/stripes case Stripes was in time to produce the disjoined section of Spots's nose, I am sorry to have to say that he was not and the facial feature has now become a former nose. You will be the first to sympathize and offer the hope that a nose by any other name will smell as sweet. And as efficient. And if you are so inquisitive as to wonder if Stripes's appeal was successful I can disclose that after corroborative testimony from a hospital doctor the disqualification was lifted. So don't run away with the idea that courts and judges are blinkered and out of touch. After all, it wasn't long ago that one of our senior judges rejected this kind of criticism by announcing that he was punctilious about keeping in touch with the ordinary people and with that in view travelled at least once every year by tube. That is an authentic report.

Before I sign off, resurrecting stories from the courts, I ought to report the case of a waiter in a Soho club who appeared at Marlborough Street charged under the Food and Drugs Act with dipping his finger in the soup he was serving. The report added that a topless waitress was charged with two similar offences.

19

PAUNCEFOOT'S LAST STAND

My time at school was fairly normal and I contend that I was a modest, good-natured boy. Please ignore declarations to the contrary that come from some of the over serious Owen's teaching staff who were unconvinced of my amazingly erudite scholarship combined with superb athleticism because my attitudes were so deceptively pragmatic and unquestioning. I have already confessed that the most exciting happening was in waiting each afternoon for the girls to come out of school in Owen's Row. It was only later in my teens that questions about the meaning and mystery of life began to trouble me and keep me awake during lessons. I was prepared to believe in fate but I was reluctant to disbelieve in luck; how else, I reasoned, can you explain the success of some of the chaps you detest? On the other hand, the insignificance and inevitability of our feeble travail in a sojourn on earth are plain to see. Great men and women through the ages have professed that our inscription in the book of life has already been precisely posted and any puny efforts on our part to influence events are nothing more than a part of the plan itself. They aver that it is not true that we make up our lives as we go along. They believe in nemesis, not luck. Admiral Lord Nelson was one of them and revealed his creed when he was mortally wounded at Trafalgar; you may not know that his dying words to Hardy were 'Kismet [note please, not kiss me'], I'm dying'. The word Kismet was misheard by a grog-crazy sailor.

Thus, the fact is that although I try to keep an open mind, I am slow to accept inchoate arguments and an encounter in California last year found me sceptical and cynically unresponsive. It was in the Polo Lounge of the pink stucco Beverly Hills Hotel, a famous watering-place, teeming with stars of stage and screen and their accountants. Especially their accountants. There were a few others who might have been flower arrangers. I was standing, trying to look like James Bond and wondering if I could afford a fruit juice, stirred not shaken, when a distinguished looking man approached. He was stetson hatted with a string tie and monogrammed boots. He introduced himself as Colonel Jeremiah Pauncefoot III of Abilene; he looked rather like a Mayfair property developer in fancy dress but not so shifty. After a polite Southern opening, he asked if I was British and if he might join me. That I was British should have been pretty obvious considering I was the only man in the room wearing a three-piece woollen suit, a deerstalker, my old school tie and brown suede shoes.

However, as I have always found that the most important changes in my life have come from the most unlikely sources and since in any case I own that I thought a free drink might come my way, I drew up two chairs and prepared to listen. The drink did indeed materialize but it proved far from free. He ordered a couple of pina coladas but tragedy struck when it came to settlement time ($28). For my part, an onlooker might have feared that I'd had a sudden paralysis of the arms so firmly were they planted in my pockets but Pauncefoot discovered to his apparent embarrassment that he'd left his wallet in his hotel suite and the only alternative to my paying the check was to make a sudden run for the door. As a man of honour and an arrant coward I rejected the latter course so that I was the one to blink first. However, any charitable feelings I had towards Pauncefoot III rapidly dissipated.

I was prepared for a species of special offer from him and thought possibly that he might try to sell me Belgium but no, it was something far more original. The colonel wasted no time and launched into a wide-ranging discourse beginning with the confession, with a great show of frankness, that he had had a drink problem (I think the problem must have been that he couldn't get enough of the stuff) but was now a three years 'dry' ex-alco. He unfolded a riveting carefully imagined account of how he had been abducted by space aliens, four feet tall with square heads, and of having been shoved into an intergalactic tube in the Mojave Desert. His story was that, before being returned to earth, they had imparted many cosmic secrets including an injection into his brain to enable him to foretell the future by reading tarot cards. He lowered his voice as he added dramatically that the secrets he'd learned were to be guarded with his life; in fact, he went on, glancing theatrically over his shoulder, he had now taken to wearing a hat at all times so that no one could look inside his head.

My reaction to this bizarre disclosure was first that it gave a whole new meaning to the expression 'brain drain' and second that we had a case here of the lights being on with nobody at home. Well, I thought it only common courtesy to hear the rest of the saga and in fact became so interested in the extraordinary tale that I hardly noticed old friends like Clint Eastwood, Arnold Schwarznegger and Elizabeth Taylor as they came up and tried to engage me in conversation. (By the way, a Hollywood agent had earlier told me that Clint Eastwood has become a dedicated opera buff and is making a film called *Die, Fledermaus*. Pauncefoot III continued his disquisition, the essence of which was that it was the future not the present that governed our survival and that he was in a position to equip me to overcome all earthly obstacles and in so doing to make a fortune. He ended with a flourish; he asked only a mere token fee of $500, a modest sum in all conscience put nominally in deference to the special relationship which subsisted between our two nations.

I had listened patiently without interrupting him but, as

he paused, it was my turn. The problem was how to repel the bounteous invitation without a lowering of the flag or a loss of face. I decided on a polemic attack as the best form of defence focused on the spectre of unforeseeability and I began by expressing my gratitude for his having singled me out as the beneficiary for such a unique opportunity. I appreciated the compliment and owed it to him to explain fully the quandary that I faced. *'Tout expliquer c'est tout comprendre'*, I twittered, brightly, to Pauncefoot. He smiled cautiously but being no linguist and sensing snags ahead, as someone once said of Peel, his smile glittered like the brass plate on a coffin. I put it to him that, of course, I was as ready as the next man to turn an honest dollar and to improve the quality of my life but I had to confess I was no dice man and I was troubled by the possibility that those wise old philosophers who for thousands of years had been preaching man's impotence to change history in the slightest degree might be right. Ergo, our life is a foregone conclusion. The colonel looked puzzled. I went on to explain that I was worried about his once-in-a-lifetime offer because, if they were right, our progression through life had already been predestined, in which event it was immutable. And if indeed they had stumbled on the true meaning of universal existence the suggested investment of $500, a not inconsiderable tranche of my heard-earned dollar reserves, might end up as of no convertible value whatsoever at Barclays Bank. In fact, some would say that I'd be better off to spend my $500 on a night out with an anglophile 38C cutie in the Playboy Club than to engage in a transfer of that sum from my account to Pauncefoot's. Especially if the cutie was a little sport who, given the choice, would be extremely unlikely to surrender the immediate certainty of some old-fashioned fun for a non-guaranteed mirage of countless millions at an unspecified future date. The fact is that I myself have always been game for a spot of culture.

I was in full flood by now and possessed him as a stoat

does a rabbit. It was cruel but I reasoned that he had asked for it. I turned on full power for the counter-offensive and marshalled what I could remember from the scripture, science and physics of my schooldays. Truth to tell, I was not renowned for my immense scholarship in those subjects. I recall painfully the occasion when Freddie Cox in charge of scripture seemed so incensed at my incuriosity about the Old Testament that his patience deserted him and he flung his personal family bible at my head; ironically, he was moralizing about the virtues of the prophet Job at the time. 'Point' Clark was in charge of science and physics and he decided that the best way to receive the inadequacy of my responses was to pretend that I wasn't there and to ignore me altogether; when he found this inconvenient on occasions such as exam time, he acted swiftly – he took early retirement. However, I did have a subsequent introduction to the theories of cabbalism and predestination through friendship with a practitioner in the field later on and this was to constitute my artillery.

I declared that the least I could do to show my appreciation was to offer the colonel an exhaustive exposition of the thoughts of the great philosophers of the world on predestination and karma, beginning with Descartes and ranging into Bertrand Russell, Schopenhauer, Wittgenstein and Terry Wogan, over the next hour or two. He hadn't bargained for this and shifted uneasily; the most disagreeable rebuff he'd had in other unsuccessful forays up to then had only been a simple refusal. I then conducted him through a litany of their teachings and bombarded him with scientific instances which, I was at pains to emphasize, were not those of solipsis. He flinched when I enquired if he had renounced supralapsarianism and if he could accept the proposition that the equation had a positive determinist factor. As a matter of fact, I said, since he was an advanced scholar in the field of metaphysics I hoped he would help demystify the epistemology and ontology aspects. Looking back, I think this challenge was the clincher, a right upper cut to the head, cruel but necessary, and I had him on the ropes. His eyes glazed over and his deep tan paled. The powerful tide of arcane language had swept away his script.

Nevertheless, to ensure an absolute quietus, I dealt him a knockout blow with an extended diatribe centred on the argument that all human action had been preordained from the beginning of time and would he not agree that libertarianism was essentially a doctrine of free will rejected by determinists? He was silent. I must confess that my own hold on the abstruse survey I was intent on laying on him had, by this time, assumed such a labyrinthine complexity that I hadn't the foggiest idea what I was talking about, but fortunately, nor had he. In any case, I'd exhausted the stock of psychobabble words I'd culled from the *Science Weekly* crosswords. Accordingly, I asked the colonel to understand my summation of a most difficult problem, namely that what I described as a marriage of complicated metapsychosis and the theosophical hypotheses with the options of sortilege or chiromancy conduced against the advisability of my plunging $500 on a rank outsider. I had intended to bang on for a bit longer but I ran out of steam altogether at this point. It mattered not because all the fight seemed to have gone from the gallant colonel; he had relapsed into a sort of torpor with an idiopathic facial twitch.

I applied some balm by assuring him that it was not that I did not trust him, only that the old joke goes 'How do you make God laugh? Tell him your plans for tomorrow.' So the proponents of the set pattern might just be right and, if so, my $500 investment would have gone the same way as most of my other investments, namely down the drain. Finally, I added with a fine show of *amour propre*, I considered myself pretty well clued up on the important areas of life, including how to work a microwave oven and how to get refunds from Marks and Spencer on returning goods that had been bought three years before, so I really had not need of casting the runes.

And anyway, he might as well know that I had some pretty powerful connections from whom I had it on the best authority (Brian Clough, no less) that the world was going to end before long if England couldn't force a draw against Andorra in the World cup, so a foreknowledge of my future in these parts would be about as much use as a chocolate teapot. I paused again and delivered what I now conceive must have been the *coup de grâce*; I offered to sell him a formula for a new hairdressing preparation that I had developed for insulating the head against intruders trying to get into a subject's mind. $528 was my price.

A little later, Pauncefoot, looking as if there had been a death in the family, rose shakily and excused himself, sobbing quietly, for a visit to the bathroom. An hour elapsed without his reappearance and I assumed that he had realized that the game was up and had either left by the back door or had been taken away to a clinic for the brain damaged. I had the satisfied feeling of having fought fire with fire and as for the $28 disbursement, I felt that I had had my money's worth. Gore Vidal once said, 'Nobody is allowed to fail within a two mile radius of the Beverly Hills Hotel.' Wrong. I hadn't, Pauncefoot had. I reached for my earthy non-insulated hat, nodded to Barbra Streisand, bowed to her accountant, and took my leave. The good colonel may have been genuine, I cannot say, but out west a man's gotta do what a man's gotta do. Of the two options, I believe I chose correctly; I still reckon the cutie at the Playboy as better value. And anyway, who knows, our date may have been an important part of her preordained career so I had no right to foul it up.

So far as Jeremiah D Pauncefoot is concerned, if he was indeed prevaricating, he perhaps learned two valuable lessons. First, it was an error of judgement to go gunning for a Brit; we are not as guileless as we seem. Second, if he had asked for a loan of $500 *simpliciter*, without all the hocus pocus and flummery, he might well have got it. I have for some time been thinking of forming a Society for Straight Talking, dedicating its members to foreswearing pretensions and calling a spade a spade and not a bloody shovel. For instance, I can think at once of one outstandingly well-qualified founder member. He is the chap who sent a letter anonymously but with fine candour to the Collector of Taxes. He wrote, 'Enclosed please find £500 for income tax. My conscience is bothering me and I can't sleep. If I still can't sleep, I'll send you the balance.' There indeed was a straight-spoken moment of truth.

So there, good readers, you have it. The age-old mystery of whether or not we can influence our lives by our actions remains impenetrable for the present. Be sure, though, the answer to this conundrum and to all the mazes of foreknowledge and fate that preoccupied the fallen angels of Milton's *Paradise Lost* will in God's good time be unlocked from the shadows of the unknowable.

20

DO PUBS SELL WALLPAPER?

Please mark that this is a cautionary tale with an object lesson. Financial considerations must never be allowed to dominate in our agenda and what's cheap is cheap. In the words of that wise Bavarian saying that my old grandfather never tired of telling me, 'It's better to go barefoot than to be without boots.' Don't ask me what it means, I'm not Bavarian and anyway, the men in the white coats came and took him away in the end. They said he was muttering something about cash flow.

The above is not to say that cash resources do not play an important part in our lives but as in every aspect of our existence, that part must be a matter of degree. The experience which I am going to recount occurred in the course of a concern for conservation of financial resources.

Readers will have noted recently that the publication of a list of Britain's Richest Men did not include my name. There is some uncertainty about the criteria laid down for inclusion but I own that the old bank balance continues fragile. It was this very morning that I had a dreadful start to the week, only too clearly out of luck; I opened the morning paper to find that I had not won £100,000 in the premium bond draw. The Disneyland holiday had gone to another, nor was the Rover car or the mountain bike mine. To compound my total eclipse, I have to tell you that I couldn't even finish the easy crossword. So as not to rise empty-handed, I was reduced to cutting out the coupon that gives me 10 per cent off the cost of a beauty care course.

The financial walls are closing in. Saint Paul's sage admonition to Timothy that we've brought nothing into this world so it is certain that we can carry nothing out is all very fine and large but he didn't have to meet his Council Tax, VAT and PAYE demands before being carried out. So I've lashed out wildly on tickets in the Association raffle; if that last hope of material relief fails, it's a choice between selling the furniture or holding up a bank.

It is as long ago as when I was seventeen, a humble articled clerk, not long left Owen's, that I felt myself slipping so inexorably out of the big money and in need of staving off bankruptcy. Those were the days when such lowly individuals as I were in receipt of no wages at all and a combination of serious amatory complications with the development of an extravagant lifestyle involving an addictive profligacy for luxuries like Cadbury's fruit and nut and Fanta lemonade were leading to a financial crisis. I needed to curb this mode of high living or alternatively find a new source of income. It is true that a Lucullan 'special' lunch at Lyons' Corner House of two poached eggs on toast, an individual apple pie (hot, if preferred), a crusty roll and butter, and a pot of tea, was then setting me back no more than one shilling plus twopence tip. Now, in the golden age, the goalposts have been moved and you'll soon be lucky if you can buy a pint of beer, a bag of crisps and a packet of 20 (cigarettes) and still have change out of a ten pound note.

Well, then, with the Hermitage Alma Mater exhortation still fresh in my ears, *'Labor Omnia Vincit'*, I elected to seek supplemental work that carried remuneration, namely moonlighting help with his deliveries for Dai Evans the milk roundsman at a weekly increment of ten shillings. It was thus that I became solvent and joined the moneyed ranks but it was short-lived. One foggy day, I misjudged the distance and backed Dai's horse and cart into a lamppost with the result that broken milk bottles were strewn all the way down New North Road and the horse became neurotic, took against me and refused to eat up unless I was out of the way. Dai gave me the sack.

Now, many years later, faced once again with an urgent regard for capital, this time to repair and redecorate my cottage in a straitened economic climate, my problems were less easily solved. The burning question was whether to give the work to an old-established building firm or to a cheaper decently modest 'one man' entrepreneur. I agonized and sought the wise counsel of an old friend, Percy McTrott, a long-time adviser on household maintenance as well as money saving in the same connection, a man who could have been a direct descendant of the legendary Mr Micawber and a senior officer in the 'Many a Mickle Makes a Muckle' brigade. Let me give you a fuller description of this remarkable man. Percy is a firm non-believer in the gospel that there is no such thing as a free lunch. He claims to have ordered his life by subscribing to the Eleventh Commandment, to wit 'never, but never, buy anything retail'. His favourite song is *The Best Things in Life are Free*. He won't admit that he is a cheapskate but confesses that in Dickens's *Christmas Carol*, he originally thought that Scrooge was the hero until he had a change of heart. He must have been the prototype of whom Damon Runyon said, 'any time you see him he is generally by himself because being by himself is not apt to cost him anything'. He is a man of few words and reminds me of the taciturn President Coolidge of whom the story goes that a woman seated next to him at dinner said to him, 'Mr President, I bet a friend of mine ten dollars that I would get at least three words out of you this evening,' to which he replied, 'You lose.'

So you will see that Percy McTrott was the ideal provenance for advice. He asked me two or three brief penetrating questions such as whether my overdraft was at its limit and if I had a second mortgage and then turned to his computer with details of my income and outgoings, at which the dreaded machine printed the laconic words,

'Are you joking?' He swiftly pronounced the case as one for a cut-rate contractor.

Truth to tell, in fairness, it did cross my mind that I might undertake the work myself but I dismissed that notion outright after recalling that the last time I tried my hand at decorating, domestic warfare in my household reached a new height and the wife packed and went home to her mother.

Belt-tightening was clearly the order of the day and Percy's advice was sound, yet I recalled the old maxim that what's cheap is cheap, not to mention all the other clichéd tips that come from wiseacres who are wealthy enough not to have to cut corners. I saw my options clearly; on the one hand, I could live with chunks of concrete falling from the roof, rain flooding into the upper rooms and a profusion of minor plagues like colonies of ants invading through cracked walls, or on the other, a monstrous disruption and crippling expense of redecoration works. Shades of Scylla and Charybdis! I caved in, reached for the local paper and turned to the 'cowboy' section.

Strategically placed between the Building and Decorating and Personal Loans columns was an ad that caught my eye. 'Quality work at competitive prices, all guaranteed 30 years. Civilized. Confidential references', it ran. I never did discover by what ancient standard the advertiser offered himself as civilized; did it mean that he will only drink your best Chateau Petrus 1961, paint to the strains of the Brandenburg Concerto No. 5 in D and takes marmalade with his bloater for tea? As to the word 'confidential', I was puzzled. I have learned to be wary of references and approach them with caution ever since I received an application from Calcutta for a senior clerical job accompanied by a reference wherein it was stated that, 'Jag Lal Singh has worked for me for two years in which time he has performed his duties entirely to his own satisfaction.' I also bear in mind the equivocal element illustrated by the classic case of the captain who wrote of the naval officer, 'This man has been known to return aboard drunk.' The man protested and the captain altered his comment to, 'This man has been known to return on board sober.'

I telephoned the advertiser and at nine o'clock the next morning Dennis appeared at the door. His last name was Adcock or Oddcock or something similar but I never did find out because he was careful never to sign anything, nor had he any bills with a printed name on them. He was extremely unlovely, a big heavy fellow, louche, looming and bull-necked, wearing, rather incongruously I thought, a red bandanna around his head; it crossed my mind that it was more appropriate to an Indian than a cowboy. He had the solid beer gut that distinguishes darts players from ordinary humans, with hands like two bunches of bananas. I hope I have conveyed to you that he was not exactly a matinée hero type. With customary shrewdness, I quickly concluded that he was unlikely to be found propagating the gospel that the meek shall inherit the earth. What I mean to say is that to be honest, I didn't care much for him.

His mate was a sallow-faced youth with earrings who played a lugubrious Stan Laurel to his master's Oliver Hardy. It later became apparent that this analogy may have been unfair to Stan because the young man proved to have the intellectual power of a Canada goose. Throughout the entire exercise of which I write, he reminded me of the famous description of the Vice President by a recent UK president, namely that if his brains were gunpowder he wouldn't have enough to blow his hat off. At all events, Dennis, a burgher from the Caledonian Road, took a pencil stub from behind his ear, wetted it with the tip of his tongue and made some mystic entries in a small red book with Islington Borough Council printed on its cover, after which he came up with an estimate for the work which he emphasized was given 'subject to contingencies'. The figure was less than crippling and I congratulated myself on having sought advice from the McTrott oracle.

The troubles began on the Monday following when a beat-up van with gay dollies dangling in the front and back windows, of a type last used as a relief ambulance in World War II, drew up outside. Dennis had only been on the premises ten minutes when he made three requests. The first was to ask if he could have half his money up front as the work was to take four weeks. I thought this somewhat cheeky and said so; after some heated debate we settled at one quarter. I was uneasy and his second request did nothing to quieten my nerves; he asked if I had an extending ladder as he had loaned his to a friend who was temporarily 'not available'. This done, he completed his requisition agenda by asking to borrow the builder's best friend, a transistor radio, specifying a make with robust volume ('We might be in anuvver part of the 'ouse'). My satisfaction at having negotiated a favourable deal was beginning to ebb.

The ensuing weeks were a period of suffering that can only be appreciated by those readers who have endured a similarly hellish experience. The frequent disappearances for days on end ('Me missus is laid up wiv the quinsies'), the dust-sheets that only covered a half of the floor area and were in any case dustier than the floors, the muddied carpets, the incessant pop cacophony of the radio, the desecration of our toilet facilities, the destruction of a much-cherished crystal vase, blobs of blood on a Chinese carpet, all combined to transform our cottage from a much-loved home into a place to which we dreaded to return. The level of whisky in a bottle of Glenfiddich on the sideboard, full at the beginning of the week, was mysteriously shrinking daily until we took appropriate remedial measures. Let me give you a useful tip in this connection that may be helpful if you happen to find yourself in a similarly oppressed situation, as follows. In the morning, lace the whisky with a goodish dose of an old Carpathian liquid laxative that does not affect the colour or the taste of the spirit but is powerful enough to move constipated horses. The results of this treatment were so dire as to be risible but even that stratagem backfired, if you'll forgive the expression, because Dennis and factotum spent a major part of the day (and the night, I hope) in urgent occupation of the bathroom instead of on the job. Anyway, the last half of the bottle remained unconsumed and was transferred to the drinks cupboard for use if another emergency arises.

Dennis and his pathetic mate vanished from the house from time to time in mid-morning, allegedly to purchase supplies of paint and paper. Do pubs sell such things? I only ask because on more than one such occasion I spotted their van in the car park of the nearby Bull and Bush. It was easily recognizable by the clouds of black exhaust smoke that belched forth from it. Our neighbours had already begun to make pointed comments about lead poisoning. The wallpaper Dennis brought back seemed to me of an unusual shade and texture, almost as if it had lately decorated another wall somewhere, but Dennis said this was only because 'nowadays all that stuff's made out of recycled paper, mate, innit'.

Meanwhile, as is her wont, the wife continued to ferry out regular supplies of mugs of tea, cheese sandwiches and generous plates of shortbread biscuits. She seemed to have got them confused with the homeless down the road. National sales of tea bags soared dramatically. At one point, I was seriously thinking it would be cheaper to hire a contract caterer. If they were grateful, Dennis and Stan betrayed no sign of it. In fact, I had one shenanigan with Dennis that threatened to turn quite ugly. I had summoned the courage to ask, very politely, if he'd mind refixing the television aerial which he'd removed from its moorings; you'd have thought I'd asked him to re-roof Stonehenge. He reacted with all the grace of a taxi driver whom you've asked to take you to Finchley when he's on his way home to Streatham at one in the morning. He looked at me more in shock than disbelief much as Ted Heath might if Margaret Thatcher asked him for a kiss.

Obviously, supererogation wasn't in his customer relations manual. I retreated in disorder. To be frank, I get nervous when I'm in a discussion and the other fellow grips me by the throat. It became clear that a logical presentation of my side of the argument might have upset him and could have led to a rearrangement of my facial features with an urgent transfer to the Royal Free Hospital. After that episode, I always kept my reading glasses on when in discussion with him in the hope that he'd be gallant enough not to hit an older man wearing glasses.

Morale at the cottage had sunk to a new low, aspirin supplies had run out, I had lost the will to live and my lady wife was on the verge of a nervous breakdown. She gave me an ultimatum; I was going to have to choose between Dennis and her. I was thinking this over when at last, seven weeks after the start, Dennis presented a bill for a sum ('to include extra materials, contingencies and rise in the cost of living index') which was nearly double the original estimate. Additional costs due to the Bosnian war were not mentioned, probably an oversight on the author's part. When I pointed out the variation from the original estimate, he snapped peevishly with a rum kind of logic that was as devastating as it was disingenuous. 'Of course it's higher than the estimate, mate. How much work do you think I'd get if I gave high estimates?' Quite so. 'And by the way,' he supplemented, 'I'll have the money in readies, if you don't mind, squire.' I swallowed the imputation about the unsoundness of my cheque and capitulated, whereupon they finally departed. Who knows, perhaps one day I'll recover the ladder which they took with them. Yes, I know I could have asked for it back but such temerity could have seriously damaged my health so I slunk cravenly back indoors.

We sat down and had a good cry. The works had cost us more than our old-established builders had quoted and we were left with the necessity of hiring a roofer to deal with the new cracks which had appeared on the roof, an electrician to see to the lights which had fused and a plumber to cure a hammering noise in the pipes that made the bathroom sound like Fingal's Cave. As for Dennis, try as I will, I cannot in all charity bring myself to believe that he is a valuable member of our community; the latest news we have of him is that he is still in residence in Caledonian Road but now at Her Majesty's pleasure in Pentonville Prison, after an incident which involved another gent in the Duke of Clarence pub. The jury could not accept that it was an accident when a pint glass in Dennis's hand collided with the other chap's face. Seven times. The mind boggles at what he might have done if he had not been civilized.

So that's another of life's lessons learned, namely that economy drives and attempts to save money for old age exact their own price. Never again. But I have to run now; I absent-mindedly took a swig of that doctored whisky this morning and can't stop.

21

RETIRED, DEEPLY HURT

This is a sad story of compulsory retirement. In opening the dissertation, I would concede that the history of cricket has its fair share of stories, of which a favourite is that related by Jonathan Rice concerning the score-book for a first-class match at Lords that bore the entry for one batsman 'retired hurt (dead mackerel)'. Subsequent readers have assumed this to derive from the scorer's sense of humour but I can confirm that it was a factual account of the retirement. It resulted from an incident when a seagull swept down into the sea lions' enclosure in the nearby zoo and stole a dead mackerel. It flew off and dropped the dead fish onto the batsman's head, causing his removal from the pitch.

My own farewell appearance was no less tragic – it was a desperately cruel story, a mixture of spiritual failure and physical pain. How unbearably sad it is when the time comes to hang up one's rig for the last time. I know because I reached that milestone and it was borne in on me that what I had suspected for many years was true, namely that cricket is the greatest game of all. The realization that I had come to the end of my active cricket career was dreadfully painful and I had determined at least that it would be a glorious final appearance. The story of that last sally in fact turned out to be strange, even bizarre, and left me deeply hurt on my departure.

Be warned, reader, do not read on if you are easily upset when faced with one of life's major tragedies, for how fragile are our carefully laid plans and how pathetic our grand aspirations. What was intended as a brilliant farewell, to the acclamation of my fellows and the watching crowd as I left my footprints in the sands of time, crumbled spectacularly into dust.

And this is the extraordinary part, the failure resulted curiously and unexpectedly only through an insufficiency of attention to the subject of geometry which I should have been absorbing in the Fourth Form. I shall explain later.

Meanwhile, I made an announcement in the clubhouse at Coopers Lane that the following Sunday was to see my final appearance on the cricket field. Truth to tell, there were no reports of panic at Lords and prices on Wall Street were firm after an initial fall. In fact it seemed to me that the news evoked a reaction that ranged from indifference to apathy but after I gave it more thought I realized that this was the stiff upper lip way in which my fellow Owenians masked their true emotions – it wouldn't do to have grown men breaking down and sobbing in the dressing-rooms. Indeed, there was a touching display of relief among many sportsmen who had been concerned for my well-being in a game with a hard ball. One had suggested, well-meaningly I guess, that I might turn to a less dangerous sport like bungee jumping.

I took the precaution of submitting myself to a strict get-fit programme of diet and exercise over some days but it was a strategy with only limited success akin to that of the chap who adopted the programme he'd heard of for eating oysters for their aphrodisiac properties. He complained afterwards that he'd eaten a dozen but only four had worked. In my case, my regime had similarly lifted my expectations but had sadly done little for my athleticism. At all events, Sunday dawned with the typical drowsy beauty of an English summer's day, namely grey, cold and wet. The sight of me in shrunken sweater, faded peaked cap and *démodé* wide trouser bottoms evoked a strong whiff of nostalgia in the dressing-room. I ignored the uncalled-for comments from one or two of the less respectful lads such as, 'Where's your zimmer, dad?'

Sheltering in the pavilion were a number of old and valued friends and intimates who had journeyed to be in at the death, so to say, some from quite distant parts. They were an ill-assorted lot and included my wife's Uncle Charlie, a sporting type, who had closed his fish and chip shop and travelled all the way from the Old Kent Road. I think he must have had a hard journey and judging by his consumption of lagers at the bar before we started, was jet lagged. This theory was supported by the fact that he forgot to pay for them. He then vomited and fell asleep. He'd brought his camp son, Elvis, of whom I can only say that at first inspection you'd have taken him for a ventriloquist's dummy.

My brother-in-law Bert had come from Chicago and by special request had checked his gun in at the bar. There was also my cousin Maude, dressed like Spandau Ballet, of generous cleavage (that did not pass unnoticed among the Owenians in the bar), a keen lady cricketer and a gregarious soul, renowned for her ample, generous and accommodating nature; what with the complicated system of the new PAYE taxation codes, she was now sleeping opportunistically with an accountant. My next door neighbour Sid brought his wife and two disagreeable offspring, clearly earmarked for reform school at an early date. Sid came along on the basis that if there is no such thing as a free lunch, a few drinks wouldn't do any harm. Even Preston Hale, the icon of Old Owenian cricket, looked in. I was particularly flattered by this because after I first joined the club, I'd been there two years before he'd deigned to notice me and permitted me to genuflect and pass the jam. Which wasn't too easy from a kneeling position. Among a few others was an old chap in a raincoat whom I didn't know nor, so far as I could find out, did anyone else. He drank up heartily. When he became truculent later and was persuaded to leave, further enquiries revealed that he'd come in and on seeing some of those present had assumed it was a meeting of the Potters Bar Time Share Tout Association.

The winter had not been a good one for me. Winters in this country can be hard and destructive as was illustrated by a recent piece in the *Stirling Observer* wherein the Chief Constable is reported as having said of a spate of indecent exposures, 'I am not concerned. They tend to drop off in the winter.' In my case, I had been away in hospital for two successive spells in the winter, the first for labyrinthitis with acute dehydration and the second a few weeks later for angioplasty on a thrombosed left leg. Hence, I was less superbly fit than usual at the opening of the cricket season. My batting average in recent times is no business of yours but had truly not been memorable; it was up to three figures, 2.56 as I recall. It certainly had been affected adversely by a habit I had developed of collapsing of extreme fatigue after being on my feet for more than ten minutes. However, it was August now and I'd reached the age when I read the *Telegraph* obituaries in the morning and only if I'm not in them do I order breakfast. So I felt that I was not senile (I told myself in fact that I had only just entered mid-life crisis).

The fixture was against an opposing side both strong and keen and a testing game was in prospect. Keith Freeman was our captain and the side included such noted figures as Williamson, Everton, Hunter, Rowswell and the Tylers. Freeman won the toss, elected to bat and put me down at number eight. Presumably, his plan was for me to hit a quick 50 if we were prospering or to mount a stolid rearguard defence if we were not.

As it turned out, after a shaky start we were 140 for 6 when I stepped out of the shade of the pavilion onto the catwalk. The heavy clouds had given way to blinding sunshine and I marched to the tumbrels. The *tricoteuses* who were sat knitting in front of the clubhouse interrupted their labours to mark my fine triumphal entrance with a sprinkling of applause, at which Uncle Charlie woke up. I didn't want to disappoint them because as

Maude said, somewhat indistinctly, they regarded me as a cult, but I was uncomfortably aware that they were looking for a pulsating performance as a final flourish to ensure a place in the Owen's hall of fame. They would probably settle for a half-ton to make the journey worthwhile. For myself, I was slightly less ambitious; taking into account weight for age, I felt that double figures would be honourable enough.

It was the end of the over and I was grateful for the respite while my colleague at the other end played out the six balls quite quietly. I then took a crouching guard with careful precision and, for the benefit of the spectators, authoritatively, imperiously and with exquisite fastidiousness, I manicured the pitch by removing one or two minute specks of grass off a good length. I then looked around, twiddled my bat professionally as I had seen Gatting do, and prepared to face the first ball. Alas, it was at this juncture that I completely omitted to remember the vital geometrical factor which could have saved me later. The proceedings were held up while three or four people continued a discussion at the bowler's end and as they melted away to positions in the field, I saw that there had been a change of bowler. They had wheeled on a chap whom I'd earlier noticed in the field. It would have been impossible to avoid noticing him for he had a 48-inch chest and size 14 boots and closely resembled Curtly Ambrose except that he was much bigger, meaner and more bad-tempered.

He had the kind of face you normally see on the wanted notices outside the police station; he had the look of a serial murderer, if ever I saw one. I noticed with apprehension that his boots were in fact badly torn open, looking as if they'd been accidentally dropped in the washing-machine, the insignia of the very fast bowler. He tried one or two sample deliveries to his slips before he got down to the serious business of placing his field. I did not in fact see these deliveries but I'm sure they left his arm because I heard them thwack into slips' hands and saw them wringing their arms as if in great pain. I observed that he had six fielders in the offside, close-catching position and the wicket-keeper had stationed himself some 15 yards back. I saw all of this and felt an icy hand clutching at the pit of my stomach as Ambrose walked back to a mark for a run-up of some 25 yards. I'm not saying I was scared, I was petrified. As my wife confirmed later when she attended to my laundry. The wicket-keeper crossed himself and the umpire called, 'play'.

His first ball was a 'sighter'. Again I did not see it. It might just as well have been a hand grenade. His subsequent deliveries consisted of a variety of balls sprayed all round the wicket like a twelve bore. I should have been grateful for the inaccuracy but I wasn't and for three reasons. First, they were travelling at about 120 miles per hour, second, they were potential instruments of serious bodily harm, and third, I was incapable of seeing them because of my failure to recall my geometry and the instruction about the law of trajectory that I had learned, or should have done had I not been so idle, at school.

It was a brilliantly sunny day by now and when the ball left the hitman's hand it was well above the top of the sight-screen, probably some eight feet high, and came at me from the very epicentre of a dazzling sun, from that point describing a downward course towards me, crouched with my head about five feet above ground. In these conditions, there was not the slightest chance for ordinary human vision to pick out the ball in the air or indeed to judge its whereabouts. In fact, as I stared straight and intensively into the summer sun, the only effect on me when the ball was delivered and began its descent towards a point between my eyes was to trigger off a severe attack of migraine.

Now, as is well known to the reader, geometry is defined *inter alia* as the branch of mathematics which deals with the properties of lines and angles; you probably discuss this well-known concept with your partner over breakfast every day. Thus, if I had been more concerned with Pythagoras in Jesse Smith's maths class and less with savouring an unexpurgated copy of *Lady Chatterley's Lover* under my desktop while at the same time poking Louis Gattenberg and Len Mitchell in the rear end with the point of a compass, I would have had the good judgement and foresight to stand erect at my full height (!), looking the bowler straight in the eye. After all, no less a coach than Saint Paul in his letter to Titus stressed the virtue of being upright. As established by Euclid's Projective Anti-Rocket Theorem, this stance would have procured the flattening of the path described by the projectile at a constant angle. Come to that, I could also have taken the precaution of planting a clove of garlic in my pocket before coming to the wicket.

Ambrose's aim was wild, as I have said but he was launching a succession of short-pitched bouncers none of which I was able to connect with. At last, obviously never having heard of the late Bill Alley's advice – 'Never bowl a full toss, even to your granny on her birthday' – he let go a full toss, chest high. I decided it was now or never and that if I was to go I would go heroically, so disdaining niceties of footwork of any kind, I struck out wildly with what can only be described as an unclassical swipe. I once saw Devon Malcolm successfully play a similar shot. It was time to make some sort of impression for my groupies in the pavilion. I felt a connection with the bat handle and the ball flew over the keeper's head. When my vision cleared, I saw the umpire signalling a boundary. I had scored four runs.

To judge by the expletive that escaped his lips and the mixture of hatred and despair which transfigured his features, I think Curtly was a shade displeased. He appeared to be weeping. His colleagues in the slips voiced some obscenities that are only normally heard on Channel 4. In fact, I was thankful that the rest of the Old Owen's team were in the pavilion out of earshot for it is well known that they are not used to rough language of this kind and are apt to be easily shocked. Nevertheless, I lifted my bat in modest insouciance in acknowledgement of the desultory clapping which came from the pavilion, and ignored the bowler. The applause was coming from my brother-in-law who was not familiar with the ethics of the game and in fact doesn't know the difference between an off-break and a prawn cocktail. His cricket lore extended only to a knowledge of the odds being currently offered by Ladbroke's on the Test Match.

Ambrose's mood had noticeably darkened and his next ball was fired with malice, aimed at my cardiac region, but I succeeded in deflecting it by brushing it with my glove. It was pouched by the keeper who emitted a deafening shout. I turned away and as I noticed out of the corner of my eye that the umpire's arm was beginning an upward arc, I started to rub my upper arm vigorously. The message was heeded, the umpire weakened and checked his arm movement. The bowler's response was swift and unequivocal; he laid an immediate curse on the umpire's entire family.

I was expecting a hostile follow-up but I shall go to my grave swearing that the next ball was not bowled but was fired from a cannon. What is more, it was in my opinion delivered from a point at least two yards over the crease; in fact, I thought Curtly was going to shake hands with me, not bowl at me. I call in evidence that the ball struck my box with a horrible metallic clunk that was clearly heard in Potters Bar High Street.

In the words of the Bard, it was 'a hit, a palpable hit'. It was several minutes before I recovered and resumed breathing. I then saw to my astonishment that the umpire, who had been standing nearer mid-off than the wicket, had extended his finger heavenward on an LBW appeal from the bowler and an early bath beckoned.

I was smarting at the injustice as I returned to the pavilion. As I passed the umpire on my way back, a dour stolid Yorkshireman with a *circa* 1923 panama hat and an anti-Southern bias, I couldn't forebear to observe, for some reason lapsing into his local patois, 'You want your eyesight testing, that were never out.' His reply was the equivalent of, *'Tot homines, tot sententiae'*; what he actually said was, 'Oh no? Tha' look in t'bluddy book, lad. Booger off.' As I marched off, I could understand and sympathize with the motivation of the Notts batsman who was recently charged and jailed for causing bodily harm as he reversed his car at the umpire who had given him out LBW.

The mood among my claque was sombre, more suited to a wake than a unique sporting occasion. After all, they had been mildly surprised to hear that I was still alive and had come to see if the rumour was true about a man in his dotage continuing to run about the cricket field as if he'd undergone some mystical rejuvenation process. They were shaken now but offered sympathy and support and declared their intention to stay on so I felt rather less downcast. Until I glanced at the score-book. I was shattered by the revelation that against my name there stood unmistakingly a duck. Nil, nought, sweet FA. My four runs had been put down to byes by the moronic bimbo who was looking after the scoring and who turned out to be the girlfriend of the opposing bowler. Is it being uncharitable to suggest that the effect of this error in improving his bowling analysis played a part in its commission?

The curtain rose on Act II of the human drama in which I was set to demonstrate the agility and grace of a gazelle coupled with the lightning speed of a swooping hawk, after a tea interval that was notable for the manner in which young Elvis distinguished himself. He tucked in with a gusto that was worthy of Les Williamson in his prime and attacked the jam puffs and the buttered scones as if it was a Harrod's sale. The session began promisingly when the giant bowler, now my sworn enemy, opened his shoulders in the second over and drove the ball like a rocket towards me at cover point, where I was still quietly brooding on my summary removal with the bat. On an impulse born of self-defence, I cupped my hands and took a blistering catch that brought tears to my eyes but was so deeply satisfying a success that I forced a smile and made nothing of it. I once saw Denis Compton do the same most effectively. I prayed that no bones were broken and the feeling would come back to my hands before I got home and had to report any damage to the wife.

The success proved my undoing. The incoming batsman struck the next ball past me towards the boundary and I raced after it to come face to face with the barbed-wire fence. At this point, with my locomotion at high speed, euphoric at my success and acutely conscious of the need to impress my visitors, my ego took over and I decided to continue my run and vault the fiercely mucronated barrier. It didn't seem difficult, I'd seen it done frequently on television. I've seen Daley Thompson do it dozens of times.

I realize now that I overlooked a basic factor, namely that my maximum leap was no more than about one half the height of the fence with the result that although I launched myself with the impetus of a *Red Rum*, I only succeeded in impaling myself firmly on the wire. Frantic efforts to fight free only resulted in severe laceration of hands and arms and I was only able to disentangle myself with the aid of a concerted lift-off by my colleagues. My discomfiture was not mitigated when they let me fall onto the far side heavily into a large fresh cow pat.

There was a good deal of visceral damage, with the crotch area once again specially targeted and I must have made a pathetic figure as I limped back to the clubhouse dripping a trail of blood. Fortunately, when I reappeared after first aid I found that my supporters had gone home, probably in shock at the failure of their hero. There wasn't much I could say, particularly since the pitch of my voice seemed to have risen by a half octave or so.

After attendance at the local hospital for an antitetanus injection and a period for healing the physical and mental scars, I recovered. However, there will be no further attempt at an epic farewell appearance.

I give notice that I'm hanging up my boots and my box and retire hurt, deeply hurt.

Finita la commedia.

22

A PRIDE OF TRENCHERMEN

I'm worried. Can my wife be trying to murder me? It's called death by cholesterol, uncommon among expert murderers but just as lethal as shooting or poison. This situation has not come about through anything I have done; it's simply that she is a superb practitioner in the art of *haute cuisine* and sets before me a succession of delectable dishes from her kitchen in the full knowledge that I cannot summon the will to walk away. I concede that they are all prepared with love and cookery is supposed to be the second oldest profession (no offence, dear) but, note please, must every dish have a massive overdose of dairy butter and double cream? After all, I am only human and my defences are down. The latest bulletin is I have slipped into a torpor of complete submission. Even a token feeble show of resistance has crumbled in the face of huge helpings of egg-rich pudding. I have pleaded, cajoled and threatened, but to no avail. Mrs Kershen is unmoved. It's something she learned from my late mother-in-law who would prepare a special gourmet lunch as the brokers' men collected up the furniture for unpaid rent. And would invite them to join the table before they whisked it away.

I've sought help but have been disappointed to find little sympathy from fellow Old Owenians. This is in spite of a little-known fact that although the alumni have made a considerable mark in various fields, notably for example in the law, banking and insurance, they also have a formidable record as trenchermen and women. If there had been a Nobel Prize for Eating, I have no doubt that some of our boys and girls would have been honoured. Many boast expertise in comestibles and are to be seen in the most exclusive purlieus. One Old Owenian, well placed in the City, thinks nothing of lunching regularly at the Ritz. As he puts it, pragmatically, 'The Ritz is a jolly good little place for lunch and meeting people and nice and handy because you can get to it on a Number 11 bus.' Not that it's essential to resort to exclusive habitats; these are just one end of the spectrum. At the other end and just as convivial, good pub food has its place among our brethren's taste. (In fact, as has been said, I've found that the best way to meet people is to pick up someone else's beer in the pub.)

Another example in the spectrum was where the late ex-honorary Owenian, Tommy Cooper, who, although a great trencherman, had to endure the awfulness of meals in provincial theatrical 'digs'. In a lifetime of playing music-hall engagements he told of one 'theatrical landlady' who made a practice of giving her artiste guests a meal of baked beans with 'use of cruet' night after night when they returned from work. After a few days, Tommy decided that he was fed up with the beans diet and was going to tell the landlady as much if she served up the same 'treat' that night. She did so but as he poked about among the beans he found a sausage. He called down the passage, 'Here, missus, there's been a mistake, I've got a sausage in my beans.' She called back, 'No dear, I put it in. Merry Christmas.' Incidentally, he said that it was the same landlady who had put a notice in his room which read, 'If you use the chamber-pot, please do not replace under the bed as the steam rusts the springs.'

When I first crossed the Owen's School threshold as an innocent with moderate eating habits, I was surprised to find that where all other healthy young men focused their attention on educative literature like *Confessions of a Swedish Au Pair*, our chaps numbered among their talents and preoccupations, both priapic and varied, a predilection towards great quantities of food and foodstuffs. I became amazed at their voracious appetites that were almost ritual and was filled with admiration at both their expertise and their capacities. As I progressed through the school and on to the Old Boys, my wonderment grew. It is with pride that we recall the names of some of the legendary sons of Owen's like Ken Attrill, who, to this day, is the acknowledged authority on smoked salmon, Keith Freeman on sushi, and Toby Tobias on cod and chips. Then, there is the one and only John Turner, one of our most distinguished OBs. Here we have the Mozart of the mealtime, a grandee of the groaning table. Was it Brillat Savarin or could it have been John who opined, 'The discovery of a new dish does more for the happiness of the human race than the discovery of a planet'. He not so much eats his dinner, he attacks it. In a long and close friendship with him, I have never ceased to marvel at his prodigious turnover of provender, never flagging and sustained at a rate impossible to keep up with.

He is acknowledged as one of the greatest authorities and is certainly the biggest consumer of chocolate profiteroles in the Western hemisphere. John's own liver will, in due time, make a fascinating subject for investigation by medical science. But be warned; he gives his undivided concentration to the disposal of his food. Don't be so unwise as to interrupt, for this normally polite and urbane fellow will transmogrify into a horrific creature who would make a snookered Hurricane Higgins look positively cherubic.

Then, take the football and cricket clubs. Let us single out a man who was probably king, Les Williamson, ex-Cambridge blue and a distinguished member of both clubs, in whom we have one of the super trenchermen. Albeit calm and sweet-tempered in action, I have seen the quiet courteous mask drop away as he metamorphoses into a feral personality confronting his victuals. I have studied him in the pavilion week after week as he has methodically put away 'teas' that would have defeated any three ordinary sportsmen; I use the word 'teas' in quotes because a sample bill of fare would include generous quantities of crab paste, egg or cheese rolls, two or three salads (some of which he would filch away from fellow consumers who were not looking), six or seven large slices of bread thickly coated with butter and jam, a few cakes and, of course, several mugs of tea. To his disappointment, the committee refused his request for fried bread at tea. Sometimes, if catering ladies were so disposed, he would enjoy a bonus of a few scones with clotted cream. In this way, he would hope to keep the hunger pains at bay until it was time to resume the battle with his digestive system with an early evening meal of some hot sausage rolls and a few tasty pork pies. We speculated that he must have hidden in his insides one of those massive destructive machines that they have in the backs of local dustcart vehicles, to grind all the waste material to a pulp. Before resuming on the field of play, he would test the North Thames sewerage system in a brief visit to the clubhouse loo. He would then bowl 20 overs, unaffected. We were not too worried by opposing batsmen who unsurprisingly complained about their concentration being affected by the bombardment of gastric flatulence as Williamson ran up to bowl. After all, most top Wimbledon players grunt as they serve these days.

I have been keeping an eye on things and have to confess that I believe that I detect a slight falling off in Les's capacity as other contenders are appearing. At his peak, I would have matched him in the premier league against Pavarotti but I do remember that he had to beat off a challenge in the 1960s from one Jack Kirby. Jack was far from a novice but sadly left us in his prime for the great canteen in the sky, else he could have been in the running for the Williamson title. It was said of Jack that he could have hogged for England, but in my opinion the smart money would still have been on Les, even with his mouth half-stitched. Les is a professional; let's face it, if he could be induced to fast for a spell we could probably cure the Ethiopian famine crisis.

True, I recall one memory of Jack chomping away at 14 fish-paste sandwiches, a quantity of thickly buttered bread with an entire pot of strawberry jam, near to a dozen cream cakes, two large slabs of Genoa cake, several chocolate biscuits and three bags of crisps for his tea without turning a hair. After tea, before we rose to resume the day's game, Jack made a practice of going around the table to have a word with each of us, much as the Japanese visitor to London who had been told it is customary and courteous on entering a tube train to shake hands all round with the other passengers in the carriage. Only in Jack's case it finally dawned on us that the object of the courteous exercise was only to mop up any supplies that had been left. That *tour de force* in no way inhibited his appetite to assuage which we once adjourned after the game to the local café at Tally Ho Corner. Ron Nash, Dennis Elston and I shared a table with Jack and were spellbound as we watched his performance. He scoffed a half of fried chicken and chips with some spam fritters on the side in short order, after which he surveyed the table hungrily and proceeded to attack and shovel off the debris from our three plates onto his own to down the lot without fuss. Dennis had had fried cod; to our astonishment, we watched as Jack without a hint of embarrassment ate what Dennis had left, the fish's head, bones and all. 'Waste not, want not,' grunted Jack.

When he'd finished, he smacked his lips noisily and removed the debris from his teeth fastidiously with his fork. His closing observation – 'Is that all there is?' gave a whole new meaning to Peggy Lee's famous song. When the waitress presented the bill, Dennis quite reasonably suggested that Jack should pay the major part. He demurred pleading that he had a glandular disorder and was under doctor's orders to eat frequently and amply. Next day, he was as bright as a button and kept wicket brilliantly. This was a true trencherman.

In recent years, a new contender in the shape of celebrated photographer Neil Matthews has emerged from the pack. Although still a novice, this is a man who has got his priorities right. His idea of the perfect woman is one who turns into a pizza at midnight. However, there have been ugly rumours that he subsists on starvation rations during the week to ensure that he has the space for a giant intake at weekend cricket and ought accordingly to be disqualified. Just the same, I would regard him as a serious challenger to Williamson if it were not that I have doubts about the totality of his commitment; does he have the killer instinct? Against him, he was spotted recently rising from the table leaving a slice of rather ancient cheese, mushroom and anchovy pizza. True it is to be admitted that he had already eaten six slices, but on that showing he's never going to make a black belt in trencherism. Another damaging report had it that he once gave Peter Banks's dog Shep some sardine rolls from the tea table. It wasn't as if the animal even appreciated the action; the beast bit him. Neil's an up and coming ambitious youngster (not yet 60) but he needs more time. We gave him the master's test one day last summer but regrettably he failed. After a tea of eight chocolate cupcakes, a packet of custard creams and six jam-filled Swiss rolls, he confided shamefacedly to Jim Everton that he was about to throw up.

There have been many others worthy of mention. Alan Hunter, Charlie Baker, Brien 'Jock' Martin, Dick Day and Mick Hooley are some who will come to readers' minds as men who gave food high priority in the quality of their lifestyles. I was present at what could have developed into an ugly scene once when Hooley accidentally (?) spilled a pint of lager over one of the umpire's sardine sandwiches. The latter had incurred Hooley's enmity when he persistently refused to raise his finger on several ear-splitting appeals for blatant LBWs. The umpire had his own back later on when he adjudged Hooley out LBW off a ball that was nearer the square-leg umpire than the leg stump. But frankly, I rate the named gentlemen as sprinters rather than stayers in this class. Incidentally, it was Jock's lovely lady Shirley who used to provide us cricketers with those so-delicious teas week after week; belated thanks to her.

When I was a lad at school, a thousand years ago, a boy named Creamer established a reputation at lunch breaks for disposing of his own shares, seconds and any surplus spotted dicks or syrup puddings that his neighbours had been so negligent as to leave unattended. Creamer became visibly larger in form as the years went on but it still lingers in my memory that the size of his head, raffia-thatched, seemed to have outgrown his body and he always looked as if the heavy intake of provisions had polarized in his head. Both pre- and post-lunch his pockets were always bulging with toffees and other aids for warding off hunger pangs. He must have qualified for inclusion in the eclectic roll of men and women who proved themselves able to consume prodigious quantities of food. I have to add that he was another whose natural bodily processes inevitably sought escape after lunch and a succession of crunching eructations, staccato explosions and noxious effluvia came from his direction at the back of the form at not infrequent intervals. These were cravenly attributed by Creamer to another boy named Lawler, who, it must be admitted, expressed himself as proud to have achieved such dramatic impact, seated nearby. The much-loved form master Jesse Smith was hard of hearing and probably also must have had dulled olfactory senses, else he would certainly at least have opened the windows. This ingestive indulgence in no way affected Creamer's scholarship and he was a serious and brilliant student, attaining high office in Government service in latter years.

From the beginning of time, it was apparent that man does not live by bread alone but that doesn't alter the fact that as a condition of life, whatever the obstacles, eat he must. There is a story of a Jewish gangster in Chicago who was ambushed outside his mother's house and raked with machine-gun fire by a rival gang. With blood pumping from several bullet holes the dying man crawled to his mother's door and managed to press the bell. She opened the door and saw her son. After only a second's hesitation, she said, 'First, eat something.' Then I'm told of a restaurant in Hong Kong that imposes sanctions, where the restaurateur prizes his fare so highly that clients have to take a medical before they are seated in order to ensure that they are fit to consume the special dishes. So it seems that eating may actually be dangerous to health.

It can also be embarrassing. An example of the need to show restraint was when I was recently seated in a restaurant adjacent to a large, ill-mannered woman. First, she constantly deployed a loud guffaw to drown out all conversation elsewhere at the table. As she leaned across me to collect the condiments, she dipped her ample bosom in my grapefruit cocktail and knocked my cutlery to the floor. The last straw was when she stole my bread roll. I was in the process of downing some vermicelli soup with dumplings, a dish to which I am most partial, when I stood to greet another guest. As I sat down again, I saw my neighbour carrying away the remainder of my soup. I was very angry and, telling her that I had not finished, snatched the bowl out of her hand and spooned up the remaining dumplings and the vermicelli. She was taken aback at my verbal attack and, I was glad to note, seemed at last to be speechless. I resumed my seat only to find that my soup was still on the table; the soup she had been removing had been her own. Incidentally, I found the missing bread roll under the table.

The necessary preoccupation with food can even on occasion carry more bizarre consequences. For example, there's the story of the capsized boat spotted near the Pacific coast of the Soviet Union where the sole occupant told his rescuers that he had only survived by eating a cow that had fallen into the boat out of the sky in mid-

Pacific. He was promptly packed off to a mental institution. However, later, after investigation of his story, it emerged that a military aircraft about to fly from its base was held up when a cow strayed onto the runway. The crew worried about where their next meal was to come from, decided to impound the cow and drove it into their bomb bay and took off. As they reached cruising altitude, the cow became agitated and they had eventually to jettison her over the sea. She landed in the boat but succumbed to her injuries.

So, finally a word of warning. I recall that the chief finding in a recent scientific study was that sex comes as naturally to people as eating. (Perhaps the difference is that you don't have to look your best when eating.) In any case, with the utmost respect, may I urge great eaters like the aforementioned Messrs Turner, Williamson and Matthews, reputedly all of irrefragable correctness, to take care to limit their prodigality.

Bon appetit.

23

SEX AND SLEAZE

Readers cannot help noticing that the media is currently full of comment centred around (a) sexual harassment and (b) sleaze, and stories about them are thick on the ground. The public seemingly cannot have enough of it. It is therefore time for me to declare a position in these important areas.

First, as to (a) I have a strong impression that the emphasis on sexual activity used to be considerably less than at the present time and I pray in aid of this submission a little-known fact – this could be due to the rise in the consumption of marmalade. I can hear gasps of surprise from readers at this revelation but the fact is that ever since the reign of Henry VIII, marmalade has been recognized as having aphrodisiac qualities; couple that historical truth with the startling statistic that marmalade is now consumed by 77% of the population over the age of forty-five, a steady rise in the figures, and the conclusion is a *sine qua non*. I am not entirely clear exactly how we can use this finding to combat the growth of sexual harassment in the Western world but in any case, it must certainly not be used unwisely. I have in mind the unfortunate case of the ageing Sloane who heard about the marmalade technique and became over-excited at the prospect of arresting an unwelcome diminution in his libido. In the City bank where he worked alongside female colleagues, he was more noted for his sexual activity than his intellect. To lose no time in profiting from the properties of the wonder nostrum, he dashed round to Harrod's and bought a quantity of the most concentrated overproof marmalade in the store and then embarked on a daily regime of rubbing the confection into the relevant parts of his anatomy. He did not disclose the success or otherwise of the remedy but was heard grumbling about the crippling size of his laundry bills.

I have to confess that I am not an authority on the sexual harassment front and had little experience as a harassee (if that is the proper description). At school, my first and only encounter was when I was in the Lower Sixth at the hands, or rather the knees, of the history master who had been severely wounded in World War II. He made a habit of seating himself with one knee pressed hard against mine. I wasn't sure at the time whether I was dealing with a mere demonstration of affection or something more exceptionable, but fortunately the contact was never pursued to a more worrying level.

Later, at work, in my earliest days as a lowly, spotty, articled clerk, I would not have been offended if a little harassment had come my way from any of the junior typists or even from the 'surplus' uncomely senior ones, for that matter, so envious was I of my older and more boastful colleagues and so eager was I to graduate in the sophisticated stakes.

There was only one direct approach at work that I remember, when I was still a fresh-faced and pretty naïve seventeen-year-old, in the course of which I was possibly a putative victim of sexual harassment. It was one Christmas at the office party when the senior partner's secretary, 46-year-old Miss Joseph, drew me by my waistband into our musty windowless stationery cupboard. I say 'possibly' because it was dark and much fumbling went on. For all I know, she may merely have wanted to know the time. She was a mature lady with very large breasts, a fine moustache and a long chin hair to match, and weighed in at something near 15 stone. She was about as winsome as a soggy kipper. And certainly less tasty.

Taking the foregoing into careful account and having regard also for her obviously exiguous acquaintanceship with deodorants, I made my excuses and left. Young I was, but even then I was conscious that as President Truman once famously said, if you can't stand the heat you should stay out of the kitchen. And the cupboard, as well. And brother, was it hot in that cupboard. In any case, fears about contracting a social disease were looming in my innocent mind.

I knew I was likely to lose a friend but for one thing, I'd been casting a long higgledy-piggledy column of figures all the morning (no calculators in those days) and in 12 different totals I had been unable to get any two the same, so I was suffering double vision, and for another, I might have managed some modest activity to show the flag, so to speak, but Miss Joseph's chin hair tickled my nose and allied with the bug-laden atmosphere in the cupboard, it set off a violent bout of sneezing that spelled the end of any amorous enterprise. I was no longer up to it and charity lost out in the battle with self-concern. I wasn't drunk enough through the mists of Australian sherry. Sure enough, Miss Joseph was in charge of the petty cash and I noted that from that time on, my travel vouchers which, it was true, were sometimes inflated where there was a possibility for walking instead of bussing to clients while charging the firm with the bus fares, a recognized means of supplementing my pitifully small pay (sleaze?), her 'blind eye' concession was no longer extended to me. My vouchers were scrutinized and pruned with a fine tooth comb.

Meanwhile, news came from Andy, the office boy, that the senior partner, a much respected figure in the community, renowned as a great miler in his younger days, had locked himself in his office with the statuesque and ambitious postal clerk (senior partner's perks?) and was probably standing up with fortitude to a bout of harassment. On the other hand, he was a devout churchgoer and they may of course have been engaged together in a spot of Bible reading. I wouldn't know but what I did note was that the nubile postal clerk received a hefty increase in pay early in the New Year. And the senior partner had to see an osteopath for treatment on his back soon after Christmas.

Andy was congenitally opposed to work in any guise (it was suggested by the office manager that if he were to be found working we should have a plaque fixed on the wall, saying 'ANDY WORKED HERE') but he had lines to arcane and unimpeachable sources for reportage of any office scandal.

On hearing his news, I did wonder, 'Do chartered accountants do it? I supposed they do but reasoned that it would have to be clinical and they would be careful not to disarrange the different coloured pens clipped into their jacket pockets; at the same time they would of course be thinking about the impact of Section 12 (2)(v) of the Fifth Schedule of that year's Finance Act and against what client to charge out the fee billing time.

The only other sex harassment in the firm was on the part of the office cat. In those days, housed as we were in an old building in Bishopsgate where mice were a problem, it was necessary to keep a cat. He was a sex maniac and we had complaints that he was keeping the entire neighbourhood awake with his yowling when sexually aroused. We were obliged to have him neutered after which he still yowled but only in an advisory capacity.

It may be that it was my lack of early personal experience in the sexual harassment department that has had an effect on my subconscious because only last night I dreamed that I was almost guilty of sexual harassment. I was a brain surgeon and as I was in the middle of a particularly delicate operation I was approached by Michelle Pfeiffer; she was dressed in a very brief nurse's uniform, stilettos and black silk suspenders, her tunic having slipped open to expose ample cleavage, pleading with me to make love to her. For a short while, like a true gentleman, I put up a show of reluctance to compromise my

Hippocratic oath and my duty to the patient, but the decision was made for me as the dream was brought to a rude conclusion when reality in the shape of the postman woke me with a bill for Council Tax.

From evidence being adduced by the tabloid press sleuths, the incidence of sexual harassment in high places is being revealed as more rife than we had suspected. And, moreover, the rifeness is not only a present-day trend. The editor of one of our most respected daily newspapers and a nationally known figure is described by a member of his staff in a recently published book as one who, 'fornicated all over the place' and was surprised in his office with a staff member *in flagrante delicto*. The writer remarked ruefully, 'And they did not even stop when I came in.' 'This led to complaints from the staff,' he added. 'Even the owner's sacred desk was violated.'

Let us turn now to the second of the fashionable headlines, the 'sleaze' factor, in the category of illicit financial gain and corruption featuring accounts of politicians and others in trust positions secretly lining their own pockets. Even in the Corinthian world of sport, allegations are being bruited about football managers accepting 'bungs' and of Test cricketing sides being touted with bribes to lose matches. I wish it to be known in the public interest that I have never once thought of taking a present nor have I ever given inducements to the opposition to throw the game in my long term of captaining cricket sides on the Regents Park gravel pitches or elsewhere.

There was one exceptional occasion when I received an offer from a farmer whose land abutted on a village cricket ground where we were playing. One or two of us were swinging our bats to such good effect that a large number of sixes were hit into the adjoining land where, but for this unwelcome intrusion, the farmer's cows would have been quietly grazing. Or apparently, judging from the information the farmer gave in his offer, would have been enjoying the attentions of his prize bull if that animal had not been seriously disturbed by the cricket balls that were winging their way regularly towards him. I believe the man was rather excited and a little confused so that I was unable to follow too clearly the details of the offer he was making me and my team to desist from further disturbance. However, I imagine that he must have thought that I was also engaged in breeding because I'm pretty sure that I heard him address me as a breeder amongst other things, in the course of his remarks. In any case, it did not matter what ingratiation he had in mind, a gift of dairy produce or whatever, because I was not about to be tempted by whatever he was offering. So, in the interests of good will and neighbourly friendship, I merely removed my batting gloves and gave him a victory sign.

Of course, the application of the term 'sleaze' must, in many cases, be in the eye of the beholder and thus be a question of viewpoint in the last analysis, and in this light be seen differently by each commentator. The world goes around because there are, and always have been, at least two sides to a question and more than one point of view to a condition.

May it first be observed that the issue of propriety is one that has more than one aspect. What seems apparently prima facie improper may in fact be perfectly acceptable. For instance, I have many a time entertained clients or been entertained by them to lunch or dinner to enable further discussions on complex matters, purely for business or professional services. There was no element of a personal nature in the intercourse and certainly none of inducement to influence their actions. Even the stern and rarely bending old Commissioners of Inland Revenue have conceded this, the Bentleys Stokes case having in effect established the principle that the costs of such lunches are to be regarded as expended wholly, exclusively and legitimately etc.

Another instance of what may be called permissible lubrication is the monetary rewards from the police to their underworld 'informers' for tip-offs. The crime figures would swell if this practice were condemned.

That censoriousness can be carried too far as evidenced by the recent proposal for a crack-down on government expenditure by diplomats abroad. This is wrong. These costs should surely be categorized as vital for the fostering of foreign relations; it would be excessive puritanism to treat expenditure of this kind as being in the realm of bribery.

The independence of our personal standpoints and their differing nature is exemplified by the parable of the lobster and the crab who wanted to get married. The lobster's mother objected on the ground that the crab walked sideways. The couple nevertheless decided to marry and did so. After the reception, the crab walked out arm in arm with the lobster and proceeded in a perfectly straight line. The lobster's mother cried, 'But it's a miracle, you're not walking sideways.' 'I know,' said the crab, 'but I'm sozzled.'

Relativity is all. When no less a sage than Albert Einstein was once asked to define relativity, he explained, 'When a pretty girl is sitting on your lap, an hour seems like a second. When you're sitting on a red hot poker a second seems like an hour.'

My personal experience has been extensive and began as early as my school days. Here, I have to confess that I was myself guilty of backsliding. There were two occasions that I recall with shame; the first was in the Remove when I accepted a bag of Smith's crisps to help a boy named Winston by letting him copy my maths paper in the end of term exams. Serious Fraud Office readers please note, he weighed 180 lb, was particularly bellicose and had also threatened me with an ebony ruler. I was in Upper VA when I strayed again and took a shilling from a boy named Bayliss to permit him to join in a game of brag being played with Young, Ambler and Pinto which I was promoting at the back of Rees's class. Well, after all, dammit, they *were* my cards.

An encounter with sleaze of a more senior sort came my way when I was still at school in the 1930s, through my friendship with Terry, a market trader and an exceedingly amiable, garrulous chap with a fruit and veg stall in the nearby Chapel Market. There was a man who, although with a winning boyish charm that made him popular with his customers, I can see could accurately have been described as the Prince of Sleaze, now that I have learned to recognize the symptoms. It happened this way. Three or four of us used to walk through the market off Upper Street in Islington before going home after school; we were fascinated by the seedy character of its denizens and after having got to know me, one day Terry offered me a part-time job as a general help on the stall on Saturday mornings. I soon came to realize that, as someone put it fairly, he thought ethics was a county east of London. He was the sort of dealer who was in a constant battle with his creditors and regarded a written contract as a mere base from which to start negotiations. His eleventh and overriding Commandment was, 'Thou shalt never pay taxes'. He proclaimed quite unequivocally and proudly the creed, 'Never give a sucker an even break'. I would put the odds against getting the better of this shrewd operator as no better than applying for a second mortgage in Bosnia.

A typical example of his business standards was exhibited when I saw him short-changing an old lady customer one day. I had got to know him well by now and remonstrated with him, mentioning the questionable honesty and ethics of his action. He made two points in reply. First, said he, 'Listen, mate, if we all thought alike, there wouldn't be any bookmakers'. I turned this profound comment over in my mind and found it obscure as to relevance and also suggestive of a happening that in any case would be considerably less than catastrophic. Second, he capped his first pillar of wisdom with a story he recommended me always to keep in mind for the true meaning of ethics. 'Dear boy,' he said ('Dear boy' was not actually the mode of address he used but that is more suitable to a respectable essay than the vernacular he did use, a term more anatomically related). His wisdom was of the streetwise variety and he did not trouble to propound abstruse laws of planetary motion in the ordinary way but on this occasion he did treat me to a lesson on his view of human ethology. 'Dear boy, ethics, I'll tell you what it is,' he said. 'It's when two partners have a shop and a plonker comes in and buys a tie for £1. He pays the partner who serves him with a £5 note and walks out without waiting for the change. Ethics, squire, is whether the man should keep the £4 himself or give one half, £2, to his partner.'

Among the favourite shady escapades of which Terry boasted proudly were his schemes to minimize his travel overheads. He owned a fast Blue Train model Rover coupé and had no respect for the speeding laws; he explained with pride and delight that all he needed to do if stopped by the police and asked to produce his driving licence was to be sure that a £5 note was placed within its covers. If asked by the officer to explain, he would plead an accidental juxtaposition of the note with the licence in his pocket. If, on the other hand, a dishonest policeman took possession of the money without comment, his story was that no prosecution ever ensued. If travelling by taxi, especially in issue on his Saturday night stag jags when he had consumed a quantity of liquor, he explained that the procedure was simple; all you had to do was to tell the black cab drivers to switch off their meters in return for payment in cash at about one half of the normal fare.

If he was to be believed (and his fantasy surely sometimes outstripped the truth), the parties in his sleazy conspiracies included police, politicians, tax collectors and food inspectors. Whether true or not, I appreciated his generosity; I used to go home and present my mother with a bag of exotic fruit which he pressed on me when we cleared the stall. I was bound to have a grudging admiration for his enterprising *élan* but I was nevertheless not at all displeased when he was taken down a peg one day. He was in the midst of a routine to his audience advertising 'apples a pound pears' and 'peaches all fresh' when a terrier began to bark and snap furiously at him and was drowning out his fast-talking 'spiel'. He shooed it away and aimed a ferocious kick at the dog. As ye sow, so shall ye reap and I was glad to see that Terry got his reap as the animal, obviously of superior intelligence, yapped and responded by defecating on his new suede shoes.

Since the foregoing early-life education in corrupt practices, I have become aware of many cases of unprincipled behaviour, some publicly reported and others in respect of which my knowledge has been gained personally, usually professionally. It has become apparent that there is only a thin line between bribery, on the one hand, and legitimate expressions of gratitude and hospitality in the interests of and to facilitate the selling of products or services on the other.

True, there are emergencies where one has perforce to submit to sleazy demands. It was not long ago that I was living in a rented house in Los Angeles and had occasion to telephone a firm of plumbers with an SOS about a choked bathroom basin. I was told by a man on the other end that it would be two weeks before they could send assistance. Pleas as to the urgency left him unmoved but he relented to the extent that he offered to deal with the offending equipment in his own time; he would want payment in cash, he said. And, he added, he didn't make house calls. I asked him sarcastically if I was expected to bring the basin to him, to which he replied quite seriously, 'Right on, buddy.' I asked him how much he would charge; he said $300 an hour. I was in shock. I protested that I only paid my doctor $200 an hour, to which he replied, 'OK. When I was a doctor, I also only charged $200.' I was sleazed and had to submit.

Well, readers, heave a sigh of resignation. The fact is that in the last thousand years, nothing has changed except for the eagerness with which the tabloid vultures are feasting on these two carcasses. All one can say is heaven help the poor creatures on whom they laser their attention who are guilty of a double, sexual harassment and bribery both.